Say It Right in

FRENCH

Second Edition

Easily Pronounced Language Systems

Clyde Peters, Author

New York Chicago San Francisco Lisbon London Madrid Mexico City
Milan New Delhi San Juan Seoul Singapore Sydney Toronto

The **McGraw·Hill** Companies

8 9 10 11 12 13 14 15   QFR/QFR   1 9 8 7 6 5

ISBN   978-0-07-176771-2
MHID   0-07-176771-1

Library of Congress Cataloging-in-Publication Data

Say it right in French / Easily Pronounced Language Systems — 2nd ed.
      p.   cm. — (Say it right)
   Includes index.
   Text in English and French.
   ISBN 978-0-07-176771-2 (alk. paper)
   1. French language—Pronunciation by foreign speakers.   2. French language — Spoken French.   3. French language — Conversation and phrase books — English.   I. Easily Pronounced Language Systems.   II. Clyde E. Peters, Author.

PC2137.S39   2011
448.3′421—dc22   2011010675

Clyde Peters, author
Luc Nisset, illustrations
Betty Chapman, EPLS contributor, www.isayitright.com
Priscilla Leal Bailey, senior series editor
Michelle Lee, French consultant

Also available:
Say It Right in Chinese, Second Edition
Say It Right in Italian, Second Edition
Say It Right in Spanish, Second Edition

For more titles and apps, see page 179.

Perfect your pronunciation by listening to sample phrases from this book. Go to www.audiostudyplayer.com, launch the Study Player, and then select: French>For Travel>Say It Right in French.

McGraw-Hill books are available at special quantity discounts to use as premiums and sales promotions or for use in corporate training programs. To contact a representative, please e-mail us at bulksales@mcgraw-hill.com.

This book is printed on acid-free paper.

CONTENTS

INTRODUCTION

The SAY IT RIGHT FOREIGN LANGUAGE PHRASE BOOK SERIES has been developed with the conviction that learning to speak a foreign language should be fun and easy!

All SAY IT RIGHT phrase books feature the EPLS Vowel Symbol System, a revolutionary phonetic system that stresses consistency, clarity, and above all, simplicity!

Since this unique phonetic system is used in all SAY IT RIGHT phrase books, you only have to learn the VOWEL SYMBOL SYSTEM ONCE!

The SAY IT RIGHT series uses the easiest phrases possible for English speakers to pronounce and is designed to reflect how foreign languages are used by native speakers.

You will be amazed at how confidence in your pronunciation leads to an eagerness to talk to other people in their own language.

Whether you want to learn a new language for travel, education, business, study, or personal enrichment, SAY IT RIGHT phrase books offer a simple and effective method of pronunciation and communication.

PRONUNCIATION GUIDE

Most English speakers are familiar with the French word **Merci**. This is how the correct pronunciation is represented in the EPLS Vowel Symbol System.

All French vowel sounds are assigned a specific non-changing symbol. When these symbols are used in conjunction with consonants and read normally, pronunciation of even the most difficult foreign word becomes incredibly EASY!.

On the following page are all the EPLS Vowel Symbols used in this book. They are EASY to LEARN since their sounds are familiar. Beneath each symbol are three English words which contain the sound of the symbol.

Practice pronouncing the words under each symbol until you mentally associate the correct vowel sound with the correct symbol. Most symbols are pronounced the way they look!

THE SAME BASIC SYMBOLS ARE USED IN ALL SAY IT RIGHT PHRASE BOOKS!

EPLS VOWEL SYMBOL SYSTEM

Ⓐ
Ace
Ba**k**e
Sa**f**e

ⒺⒺ
See
Fee**t**
Mee**t**

Ⓞ
Oak
Co**l**d
So**l**d

⑳
Coo**l**
Poo**l**
Too

ⓐ̃
Cat
Sad
Hat

ⓔ̃
Men
Red
Bed

ⓐⓗ
Calm
Ho**t**
Off

ⓤⓗ
Fun
Sun
Run

ⓔⓦ
New
Few
Dew

This symbol represents the French letter **u**. Put your lips together as if to kiss and say **EE**.

ⓞⓤ
Could
Would
Book

This symbol represents a unique sound found in the letters **eu** in French spelling. To master this sound you must listen to a native speaker's pronunciation. The **ou** sound in c**ou**ld is an effective substitute.

EPLS CONSONANTS

Consonants are letters like **T**, **D**, and **K**. They are easy to recognize and their pronunciation seldom changes. The following pronunciation guide letters represent some unique French consonant

Ŗ   Represents the French **r**. There is no English equivalent for this sound and it is very difficult to reproduce. It is pronounced far back in the throat and will take practice. It is essential to listen to a native speaker to master this sound. This Ŗ helps to remind you of the unique French r sound.

ZH Pronounce these EPLS letters like the **s** in mea**s**ure.

KW Pronounce these EPLS letters like the **qu** in **qu**it.

Nasalized Vowel Sounds

In French certain vowels are nasalized. This (**ñ**) immediately following a symbol tells you to nasalize the sound that the symbol represents. Try pinching your nose while pronouncing these words (try not to sound the **n** in the words):

Can	Zone	On	Sun
K(ä)ñ	Z(o)ñ	(ah)ñ	S(uh)ñ

PRONUNCIATION TIPS

- Each pronunciation guide word is broken into syllables. Read each word slowly, one syllable at a time, increasing speed as you become more familiar with the system.

- In general, equal emphasis is given to each syllable. Sometimes the French will slightly stress the last syllable in a sentence.

- Most of the symbols are pronounced the way they look!

- This phrase book provides a means to speak and be understood in French. **To perfect your French accent you must listen closely to French speakers and adjust your speech accordingly.**

- The pronunciation and word choices in this book were chosen for their simplicity and effectiveness.

- Some pronunciation guide letters are underlined (**Z I N**). This is simply to let you know that the underlined letter is a linking sound (called liaison) that connects two words.

- **SVP** is the abbreviation for **s'il vous plaît** which means "please" in French. You will see it used throughout the book.

ICONS USED IN THIS BOOK

KEY WORDS

You will find this icon at the beginning of chapters indicating key words relating to chapter content. These are important words to become familiar with.

PHRASEMAKER

The Phrasemaker icon provides the traveler with a choice of phrases that allows the user to make his or her own sentences.

Say It Right in **FRENCH**

ESSENTIAL WORDS AND PHRASES

Here are some basic words and phrases that will help you express your needs and feelings in **French**.

Hello

Bonjour

BOñ ZHOOR

How are you?

Comment allez-vous?

KO-MOñ Tã-LA-VOO

Fine / Very well

Très bien

TRA BEE-ahñ

And you?

Et vous?

A VOO

Good-bye

Au revoir

O Ruh-VWahR

Good morning

Bonjour

BOñ ZHooR

Good evening

Bonsoir

BOñ SWahR

Good night

Bonne nuit

BuhN NWEE

Mr.

Monsieur

Muh-SYou

Mrs.

Madame

Mã-Dãm

Miss

Mademoiselle

MãD-MWah-ZěL

Yes

Oui

WEE

No

Non

NOñ

Please

S'il vous plaît

SEEL VOO PLĒ

Abbreviated SVP throughout the book

Thank you

Merci

MĒR-SEE

Excuse me

Pardon

PahR-DOñ

I'm sorry

Je suis désolé

ZHuh SWEE DA-ZO-LA

I'm a tourist.

Je suis touriste.

ZH(uh) SW(EE) T(oo)-R(EE)ST

I do not speak French.

Je ne parle pas français.

ZH(uh)N-(uh) P(ah)RL P(ah) FR(ah)ñ-S(A)

I speak a little French.

Je parle un peu français.

ZH(uh) P(ah)RL (uh)ñ P(ou) FR(ah)ñ-S(A)

Do you understand English?

Comprenez-vous l'anglais?

K(O)ñ-PR(uh)-N(A)-V(oo) L(ah)ñ-GL(A)

I don't understand!

Je ne comprends pas!

ZH(uh)N-(uh) K(O)ñ-PR(ah)ñ P(ah)

Please repeat.

Répétez s'il vous plaît.

R(e)-P(e)-T(A) S(EE)L V(oo) PL(e)

FEELINGS

I want…
Je veux…
ZH(uh) V(ou)…

I have…
J'ai…
ZH(A)…

I know.
Je sais.
ZH(uh) S(A)

I don't know.
Je ne sais pas.
ZH(uh)N S(A) P(ah)

I like it.
Je l'aime bien.
ZH(uh) L(e)M B(EE)-(ah)ñ

I don't like it.
Je ne l'aime pas bien.
ZH(uh)N-(uh) L(e)M P(ah) B(EE)-(ã)ñ

I'm lost.

Je suis perdu.

ZH⒰ SW㋔ P㋕R-D㋔

I'm in a hurry.

Je suis pressé.

ZH⒰ SW㋔ PR㋕-S㋐

I'm tired.

Je suis fatigué.

ZH⒰ SW㋔ F㋐-T㋔-G㋐

I'm ill.

Je suis malade.

ZH⒰ SW㋔ M㋐-L㋐D

I'm hungry.

J'ai faim.

ZH㋐ F㋐ñ

I'm thirsty.

J'ai soif.

ZH㋐ SW㋐F

I'm angry.

Je suis en colère.

ZH⒰ SW㋔ Z㋐ñ KO-L㋕R

INTRODUCTIONS

My name is...

Je m'appelle...

ZH⒰ M⒜-P⒠L...

What's your name?

Comment vous appelez-vous?

K⒪-M⒪ñ V⒪⒪ Z⒜-PL⒜ V⒪⒪

Where are you from?

D'où venez-vous?

D⒪⒪ V⒰-N⒜ V⒪⒪

Do you live here?

Habitez-vous ici?

⒜-B⒠⒠-T⒜ V⒪⒪ Z⒠⒠-S⒠⒠

I just arrived.

Je viens d'arriver.

ZH⒰ V⒠⒠-⒜ñ D⒜-B⒠⒠-V⒜

What hotel are you [staying] at?

Vous restez à quel hôtel?

V⒪⒪ B⒠S-T⒜ ⒜ K⒠ L⒪-T⒠L

I'm at the…hotel.

Je reste à l'hôtel...

ZHⓓ RⓏST ⓑ LⓈ-TⓏL...

It was nice to meet you.

Je suis enchanté de faire votre connaissance.

ZHⓑ SWⓑ Zⓑñ-SHⓑñ-Tⓑ
Dⓓ FⓏR VⓈ-TRⓓ
KⓈ-Nⓑ-SⓑñS

See you tomorrow.

A demain.

ⓑ Dⓓ-Mⓑñ

See you later.

A bientôt.

ⓑ Bⓑ-ⓑñ-TⓈ

Good luck!

Bonne chance!

BⓓN SHⓑñS

In this book the symbol ⓓ is used to represent the French letter **"e"** in words such as **le, de,** etc. To master your French accent, have a French speaker pronounce these words and try to hone your accent accordingly.

THE BIG QUESTIONS

Who?

Qui?

K①①

Who is it?

Qui est-ce?

K①①   ěS

What?

Quoi?   Comment?

KWⓐ   KⓄ-MⓄñ

What's that?

Qu'est-ce que c'est?

KěS-Kⓔ   SⒶ

When?

Quand?

Kⓐñ

Where?

Où?

⓴

Where is…?

Où est...?

⊙⊙ Ⓐ

Which?

Quel?   Quelle?   Quels?   Quelles?

KⒺL

Although spelled differently these are all pronounced the same.

Why?

Pourquoi?

P⊙⊙R KW⊛

How?

Comment?

K⊙-M⊙ñ

How much does it cost?

Combien?

K⊙ñ-BⒺⒺ-⊛ñ

How long?

Combien de temps?

K⊙ñ-BⒺⒺ-⊛ñ D⊛ T⊛ñ

ASKING FOR THINGS

The following phrases are valuable for directions, food, help, etc.

I would like...

Je voudrais...

ZHⓤⱨ Vⓞⓞ-Dℝ🅐...

I need...

J'ai besoin...

ZH🅐 Bⓤⱨ-ZWⓐⱨñ...

Can you...?

Pouvez-vous...?

Pⓞⓞ-V🅐-Vⓞⓞ...

When asking for things be sure to say <u>please</u> and <u>thank you</u>.

Please	**Thank you**
S'il vous plaît	Merci
SⓔⓔL Vⓞⓞ PLⓔ̃	Mⓔ̃ℝ-Sⓔⓔ

PHRASEMAKER

Combine **I would like** with the following phrases, and you will have an effective way to ask for things.

I would like… please.

Je voudrais... s'il vous plaît.

ZH⑩ V⑩-DℝⒶ… SVP

▸ **more coffee**

plus de café

PL⒠ⓦ D⑩ KⓐⱧ-FⒶ

▸ **some water**

de l'eau

D⑩ LⓄ

▸ **some ice**

des glaçons

DⒶ GLⓐ-SⓄñ

▸ **the menu**

le menu

L⑩ Mⓔ-N⒠ⓦ

PHRASEMAKER

Here are a few sentences you can use when you feel the urge to say **I need** or **Can you...**?

I need…

J'ai besoin... s'il vous plaît

ZH🅐 B🅤-ZW🅐ñ... SVP

▶ **help**

d'aide

D🅔D

▶ **directions**

de directions

D🅤 D🇪🇪-R🅔K-S🇪🇪-🅞ñ

▶ **more money**

de plus d'argent

D🅤 PL🅔🆆 D🅐R-ZH🅐ñ

▶ **change**

de monnaie

D🅤 M🅞-N🅐

▶ **a lawyer**

d'un avocat

D🅤ñ N🅐-V🅞-K🅐

PHRASEMAKER

Can you...

Pouvez-vous... s'il vous plaît

P@-V@-V@... SVP

▸ **help me?**

m'aider?

M@-D@

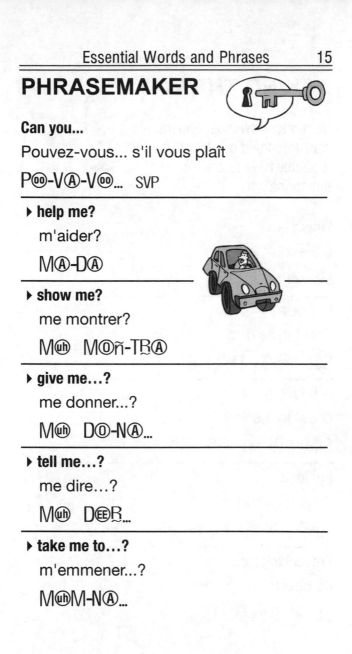

▸ **show me?**

me montrer?

M@ M@ñ-TR@

▸ **give me…?**

me donner...?

M@ D@-N@...

▸ **tell me…?**

me dire…?

M@ D@R...

▸ **take me to…?**

m'emmener...?

M@M-N@...

ASKING THE WAY

No matter how independent
you are, sooner or later you'll
probably have to ask for
directions.

Where is...?

Où est...?

⓪⓪ Ⓐ...

Is it near?

C'est près d'ici?

SⒶ PⓇⒶ DⒺⒺ-SⒺⒺ

Is it far?

C'est loin d'ici?

SⒶ LWⒶñ DⒺⒺ-SⒺⒺ

I'm lost!

Je suis perdu!

ZHⓤⓗ SWⒺⒺ PⒺⓇ-Dⓔⓦ

I'm looking for...

Je cherche...

ZHⓤⓗ SHⓔⓇSH...

PHRASEMAKER

Where is...

Où est...

⊚ Ⓐ...

▸ **the telephone?**

le téléphone?

Lⓤ TⒶ-LⒶ-FⓤN

▸ **the beach?**

la plage?

LⒶ PLⒶZH

▸ **the hotel...?**

l'hôtel...?

LO-TěL...

▸ **the train for...?**

le train pour...?

Lⓤ TRⓐ̃ PⓄR...

Where are the restrooms?

Où sont les toilettes?

⊚ SⓄ̃ LⒶ TWⒶ-LěT

TIME

What time is it?

Quelle heure est-il?

K🖽 L⓪R Ⓐ-TⒺL

Morning

Le matin

Lⓤ Mⓐ-Tãñ

Noon

Midi

MⒺ-DⒺ

Night

La nuit

Lⓐ NWⒺ

Today

Aujourd'hui

Ⓞ-ZH⓪R-DWⒺ

Tomorrow

Demain

Dⓤ-Mãñ

This week
Cette semaine
SēT Suh-MēN

This month
Ce mois
Suh MWah

This year
Cette année
SēT ah-NA

Now
Maintenant
Mãñ-Tuh-Nahñ

Soon
Bientôt
BEE-ahñ-TO

Later
Plus tard
PLew TahR

Never
Jamais
ZHah-MA

WHO IS IT?

I
Je
ZH⒰

You (formal)	**You** (informal)
Vous	Tu
V⒪⒪	T⒠⒲
Use this form of **you** with people you don't know well.	Use this form of **you** with people you know well.

He
Il
⒠⒠L

She
Elle
⒠L

We
Nous
N⒪⒪

They

Ils (m)	Elles (f)
⒠⒠L	⒠L
A group of **men** only or a group of men and women.	A group of **women** only.

THE, A (AN), AND SOME

To use the correct form of **The**, **A** (**An**), or **Some**, you must know if the French word is masculine or feminine. Often you will have to guess! If you make a mistake, you will still be understood.

The

La

L⒜ⓗ

The before a singular feminine noun:
(La) woman is pretty.

Les

L⒜

The before a plural feminine noun:
(Les) women are pretty.

Le

L⒰ⓗ

The before a singular masculine noun:
(Le) boy is handsome.

Les

L⒜

The before a plural masculine noun:
(Les) boys are handsome.

A or **An**

Un

⒰ⓗñ

A or **an** before a singular masculine noun:
He is (un) man.

Une

⒠ⓦN

A or **an** before a singular feminine noun:
She is (une) woman.

Some

Des

D⒜

Some before singular masculine nouns:
(Des) boys.

Des

D⒜

Some before singular feminine nouns:
(Des) women.

USEFUL OPPOSITES

Near	**Far**
Près de	Loin
PR(A) D(uh)	LW(ah)ñ

Here	**There**
Ici	Là
(EE)-S(EE)	L(ah)

Left	**Right**
A gauche	A droite
(ah) G(O)SH	(ah) DR(W)(ah)T

A little	**A lot**
Un peu	Beaucoup
(uh)ñ P(ou)	B(O)-K(oo)

More	**Less**
Plus	Moins
PL(ew)	MW(ah)ñ

Big	**Small**
Grand (m) / Grande (f)	Petit (m) / Petite (f)
GR(ah)ñ / GR(ah)ND	P(uh)-T(EE) / P(uh)-T(EE)T

Adjectives are masculine or feminine depending on the noun they describe.

Open	**Closed**
Ouvert (m)/Ouverte (f)	Fermé (m) / Fermée (f)
⊚-VÊR / ⊚-VÊRT	FÊR-MA

Cheap	**Expensive**
Bon marché	Cher (m) / Chère (f)
BOñ MahR-SHA	SHÊR

Clean	**Dirty**
Propre	Sale
PRO-PRuh	SahL

Good	**Bad**
Bon (m) / Bonne (f)	Mauvais (m) / Mauvaise (f)
BOñ / BuhN	MO-VA / MO-VÊZ

Vacant	**Occupied**
Libre	Occupé (m) / Occupée (f)
LEE-BRuh	O-Kew-PA´

Right	**Wrong**
Avoir raison	Avoir tort
ah-VWahR	ah-VWahR TOR
RA-ZOñ	

WORDS OF ENDEARMENT

I love you.

Je t'aime.

ZH(uh) T(ē)M

My love

Mon amour

M(O)ñ N(ah)-M(oo)R

My life

Ma vie

M(ah) V(EE)

My friend (to a male)

Mon ami (m)

M(O)ñ N(ah)-M(EE)

My friend (to a female)

Mon amie (f)

M(O)ñ N(ah)-M(EE)

Kiss me!

Embrasse-moi!

(ah)ñ-BR(ah)S MW(ah)

WORDS OF ANGER

What do you want?

Qu'est-ce que vous voulez?

KᵉS Kᵘʰ Vᵒᵒ Vᵒᵒ-Lᴀ

Leave me alone!

Laissez-moi tranquille!

Lᴀ-Sᴀ MWᵃʰ TRᵃʰñ-KᴱᴱL

Go away!

Allez-vous-en!

ᵃʰ-Lᴀ Vᵒᵒ-Zᵃʰñ

Stop bothering me!

Ne me dérangez pas!

Nᵘʰ Mᵘʰ Dᴀ-Rᵃʰñ-ZHᴀ Pᵃʰ

Be quiet!

Taisez-vous!

Tᴀ-Zᴀ Vᵒᵒ

That's enough!

C'est assez!

Sᴀ Tᵃʰ-Sᴀ

COMMON EXPRESSIONS

!!!

When you are at a loss for words but have the feeling you should say something, try one of these!

Who knows?

Qui sait?

K⒠ S⒜

That's the truth!

C'est la vérité!

S⒜ L⒜ V⒜-R⒠-T⒜

Sure!	**Wow!**
Bien sûr!	Chouette!
B⒠-⒜ñ S⒠R	SH⒪⒪-⒠T

What's happening?

Qu'est-ce qui se passe?

K⒠S K⒠ S⒰ P⒜S

I think so.

Je pense que oui.

ZH⒰ P⒜ñS K⒰ W⒠

Cheers!

A votre santé!

ah VO-TRuh Sahñ-TA

Good luck!

Bonne chance!

BuhN SHahñS

With pleasure!

Avec plaisir!

ah-VēK PLA-ZEER

My goodness!

Mon dieu!

MOñ DYou

What a shame! / That's too bad!

C'est dommage!

SA DO-MahZH

Well done! Bravo!

Bravo!

BRah-VO

Never mind!

N'importe quoi!

Nañ-PORT KWah

USEFUL COMMANDS

Stop!
Arrêtez!
@-R@-T@

Go!
Allez!
@-L@

Wait!
Attendez!
@-T@ñ-D@

Hurry!
Dépêchez-vous!
D@-P@-SH@ V@

Slow down!
Lentement!
L@ñT-M@ñ

Come here!
Venez ici!
V@-N@ Z@-S@

Help!
Au secours!
O S@-K@R

EMERGENCIES

Fire!

Au feu!

O-Fou

Emergency!

L'urgence!

LewR-ZHahñS

Call the police!

Téléphonez à la police!

TA-LA-FO-NA ah Lah PO-LEES

Call a doctor!

Téléphonez au médecin!

TA-LA-FO-NA O MA-Duh-Sahñ

Call an ambulance!

Faites venir une ambulance!

FёT Vuh-NEER ewN ahñ-Bew-LahñS

I need help!

Au secours!

O Suh-KooR

ARRIVAL

Passing through customs should be easy since there are usually agents available who speak English. You may be asked how long you intend to stay and if you have anything to declare.

- Have your passport ready.

- Be sure all documents are up-to-date.

- While in a foreign country, it is wise to keep receipts for everything you buy.

- Be aware that many countries will charge a departure tax when you leave. Your travel agent should be able to find out if this affects you.

- If you have connecting flights, be sure to reconfirm them in advance.

- Make sure your luggage is clearly marked inside and out.

- Take valuables and medicines in carry-on bags.

SIGNS TO LOOK FOR:

DOUANE (Customs)

FRONTIERE (Border)

LES BAGAGES (Baggage claim)

KEY WORDS

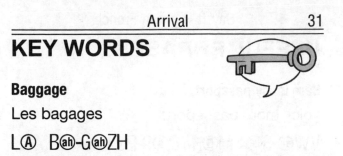

Baggage

Les bagages

L@ B@-G@ZH

Customs

La douane

L@ DW@N

Documents

Les documents

L@ D©-K©-M@ñ

Passport

Le passeport

L@ P@S-P©R

Porter

Le porteur

L@ P©R-T©R

Tax

La taxe

L@ T@KS

USEFUL PHRASES

Here is my passport.

Voici mon passeport.

VW⒜-S⒠ M⓪ñ P⒜S-P⓪ß

I have nothing to declare.

Je n'ai rien à déclarer.

ZH⒰ N⒜ ß⒠-ahñ ah

D⒜-KL⒜-ß⒜

I'm here on business.

Je suis en voyage d'affaires.

ZH⒰ SW⒠ Z⒜ñ

VW⒪-Y⒜ZH D⒜-F⒠ß

I'm here on vacation.

Je suis en vacances.

ZH⒰ SW⒠ Z⒜ñ V⒜-K⒜ñS

Is there a problem?

Il y a un problème?

⒠L ⒠ ah ⒰ñ Pß⓪-BL⒠M

PHRASEMAKER

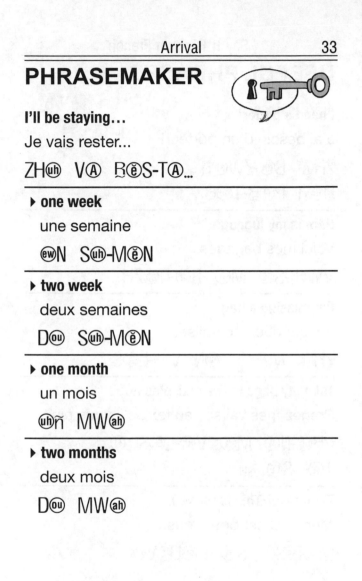

I'll be staying…

Je vais rester...

ZH⒰ V⒜ R⒠S-T⒜...

▸ **one week**

une semaine

⒠wN S⒰-M⒠N

▸ **two week**

deux semaines

D⒪⒰ S⒰-M⒠N

▸ **one month**

un mois

⒰ñ MW⒜

▸ **two months**

deux mois

D⒪⒰ MW⒜

USEFUL PHRASES

I need a porter!

J'ai besoin d'un porteur!

ZH Buh-ZWahñ
Duhñ POR-TouR

Here is my luggage.

Voici mes bagages.

VWah-SEE M Bã-GahZH

I'm missing a bag.

Je manque une valise.

ZHuh Mahñk ewN Vah-LEES

Take my bags to the taxi, please.

Prenez mes valises au taxi, s'il vous plaît.

PRuh-N M Vah-LEES O
Tãk-SEE SVP

Thank you. This is for you.

Merci. C'est pour vous.

MëR-SEE S POoR Voo

PHRASEMAKER

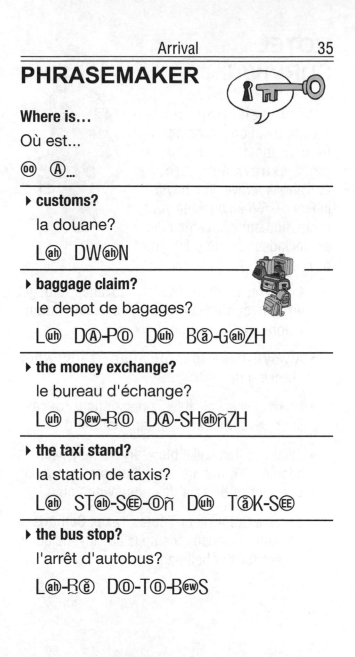

Where is…

Où est...

⑩ Ⓐ...

▶ **customs?**

la douane?

L⦿ DW⦿N

▶ **baggage claim?**

le depot de bagages?

L⦿ D④-P⦿ D⦿ B⦿-G⦿ZH

▶ **the money exchange?**

le bureau d'échange?

L⦿ B⦿-R⦿ D④-SH⦿ñZH

▶ **the taxi stand?**

la station de taxis?

L⦿ ST⦿-S⦿-⦿ñ D⦿ T④K-S⦿

▶ **the bus stop?**

l'arrêt d'autobus?

L⦿-R⦿ D⦿-T⦿-B⦿S

HOTEL SURVIVAL

A wide selection of accommodations, ranging from the most basic to the most extravagant, are available wherever you travel in France. When booking your room, find out what amenities are included for the price you pay.

- Make reservations well in advance and get written confirmation of your reservations before you leave home.

- Always have identification ready when checking in.

- Do not leave valuables, prescriptions, or cash in your room when you are not there.

- Electrical items like blow-dryers may need an adapter. Your hotel may be able to provide one, but to be safe, take one with you.

- **Service Compris** or **Toutes Taxes Comprises** on your bill means the tip is already included, except for the bellman.

KEY WORDS

Hotel Baggage

L'hôtel

LO-TёL

Bellman

Un garçon d'hôtel

uhñ GahR-SOñ DO-TёL

Maid

Une domestique

ewN DO-MёS-TEEK

Message

Le message

Luh Mё_S-SahZH

Reservation

La réservation

Lah RёE-SёR-Vah-SEE-Oñ

Room service

Le service dans les chambres

Luh SёR-VEES Dahñ LA SHahñ-BRuh

CHECKING IN

My name is…

Je m'appelle...

ZH⒰ M⒜-P⒠L

I have a reservation.

J'ai réservé.

ZH⒜ R⒠-S⒠R-V⒜

Have you any vacancies?

Vous avez des chambres libres?

V⒪⒪ Z⒜-V⒜ D⒜
SH⒜ñ-BR⒰ L⒠⒠-BR⒰

What is the charge?

Quel est le prix?

K⒠ L⒜ L⒰ PR⒠⒠

Is there room service?

Il y a le service dans les chambres?

⒠⒠L ⒠⒠ ⒜ L⒰ S⒠R-V⒠⒠S
D⒜ñ L⒜ SH⒜ñ-BR⒰

My room key, please.

Ma clé de chambre, s'il vous plaît.

M⒜ KL⒠ D⒰ SH⒜ñ-BR⒰ SVP

PHRASEMAKER

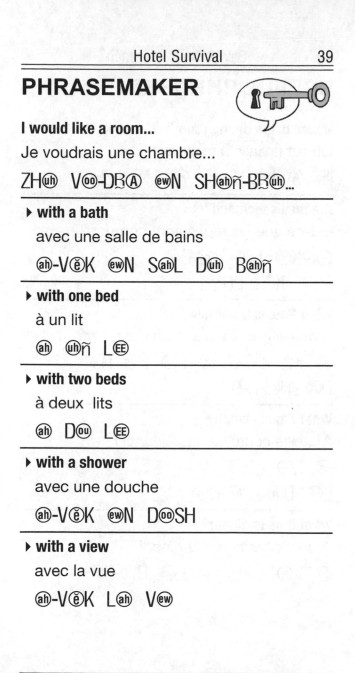

I would like a room...

Je voudrais une chambre...

ZH(uh) V(oo)-DR(A) (ew)N SH(ah)ñ-BR(uh)...

▶ **with a bath**

avec une salle de bains

(ah)-V(ĕ)K (ew)N S(ah)L D(uh) B(ah)ñ

▶ **with one bed**

à un lit

(ah) (uh)ñ L(EE)

▶ **with two beds**

à deux lits

(ah) D(ou) L(EE)

▶ **with a shower**

avec une douche

(ah)-V(ĕ)K (ew)N D(oo)SH

▶ **with a view**

avec la vue

(ah)-V(ĕ)K L(ah) V(ew)

USEFUL PHRASES

Where is the dining room?

Où est la salle à manger?

ⓞⓞ Ⓐ Lⓐⓗ SⓐⓗL ⓐⓗ Mⓐⓗñ-ZHⒶ

Are meals included?

Est-ce que les repas sont compris?

ⓔS-Kⓤⓗ LⒶ Rⓤⓗ-Pⓐⓗ

SOñ KOñ-PRⒺⒺ

What time is breakfast?

A quelle heure est le petit déjeuner?

ⓐⓗ Kⓔ LⓄⓤR Ⓐ Lⓤⓗ Pⓤⓗ-TⒺⒺ

DⒶ-ZHⓄⓤ-NⒶ

What time is lunch?

A quelle heure est le déjeuner?

ⓐⓗ Kⓔ LⓄⓤR Ⓐ

Lⓤⓗ DⒶ-ZHⓄⓤ-NⒶ

What time is dinner?

A quelle heure est le dîner?

ⓐⓗ Kⓔ LⓄⓤR Ⓐ Lⓤⓗ DⒺⒺ-NⒶ

Are there any messages for me?

Y a-t-il des messages pour moi?

Ⓔ ⓐ TⒺL Dâ Mě-SⓐZH

Pⓞ MWⓐ

Please wake me at...

Veuillez me réveiller à...

Vⓞ-Yâ Mⓤ Ṛě-Vě-Yâ ⓐ...

6:00	6:30
six heures	six heures et demie
SⒺ Zⓞ	SⒺ Zⓞ â Dⓤ-MⒺ

7:00	7:30
sept heures	sept heures et demie
Sě Tⓞ	Sě Tⓞ â Dⓤ-MⒺ

8:00	8:30
huit heures	huit heures et demie
WⒺ Tⓞ	WⒺ Tⓞ â Dⓤ-MⒺ

9:00	9:30
neuf heures	neuf heures et demie
Nⓞ Vⓞ	Nⓞ Vⓞ â Dⓤ-MⒺ

PHRASEMAKER

I need…

J'ai besoin...

ZH④ B⑩-ZW⑭ñ…

▸ **a babysitter**

d'une garde-bébé

D⑩N G⑭RD B④-B④

▸ **a bellman**

d'un garçon d'hôtel

D⑩ñ G⑭R-S⓪ñ D⓪-T⑯L

▸ **more blankets**

de plus de couvertures

D⑩ PL⑩ D⑩ K⓪⓪-V⑯R-T⑩R

▸ **a hotel safe**

d'un coffre-fort

D⑩ñ K⓪-FR⑩ F⓪R

▸ **ice cubes**

de glaçons

D⑩ GL④-S⓪ñ

▸ **an extra key**

d'un clé supplémentaire

Duhñ KLA Sew-PLA-Muhñ-TēR

▸ **a maid**

de domestique

Duh DO-MēS-TēK

▸ **the manager**

de directeur (m)   de directrice (f)

Duh DEE-RēK-TouR   Duh DEE-RēK-TRēS

▸ **clean sheets**

de draps propre

Duh DRah PRO-PRuh

▸ **soap**

de savon

Duh Sah-VOñ

▸ **toilet paper**

de papier hygiénique

Duh Pah-PEE-A EE-ZHEE-A-NēK

▸ **more towels**

de plus de serviettes

Duh PLew Duh SēR-VEE-ēT

PHRASEMAKER
(PROBLEMS)

There is no...

Il n'y a pas...

ⒺL NYⓐ Pⓐ...

▶ **electricity**

d'électricité

DⓐL-LⓔK-TRⒺ-SⒺ-Tⓐ

▶ **heat**

de chauffage

DⓤSHⓄ-Fⓐ ZH

▶ **hot water**

d'eau chaude

DⓄ SHⓄD

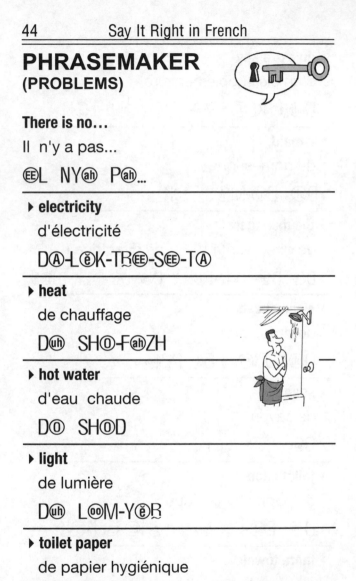

▶ **light**

de lumière

DⓤL LⓄⓄM-YⓔR

▶ **toilet paper**

de papier hygiénique

DⓤP Pⓐ-PⒺ-Ⓐ Ⓔ-ZHⒺ-Ⓐ-NⒺK

PHRASEMAKER
(SPECIAL NEEDS)

Do you have…

Avez-vous...

@-V@ V@...

▸ **an elevator?**

un ascenseur?

@ñ N@-S@ñ-S@B

▸ **a ramp?**

une rampe?

@N B@MP

▸ **a wheelchair?**

un fauteuil roulant?

@ñ F@-T@-Y@ B@-L@ñ

▸ **facilities for the disabled?**

des aménagements pour les
handicapés?

D@ Z@-M@-N@ZH-M@ñ P@B
L@ @N-D@-K@-P@

CHECKING OUT

The bill, please.

Voulez-vous me préparer la note, s'il vous plaît.

V⊚-L◯-V⊚ M⒰ PR◯-P⒜-R◯
L⒜ N◯T ₛᵥₚ

Is this bill correct?

Il y a une erreur dans la note?

Ⓔ︎Ⓔ︎L Ⓔ︎Ⓔ︎ ⒜ ⒠ⓦN ⒠R-⒪R
D⒜ñ L⒜ N◯T

Do you accept credit cards?

Acceptez-vous les cartes de crédit?

⒜-S⒠P-T◯ V⊚ L◯ K⒜RT
D⒰ KR◯-D⒠⒠

Could you have my luggage brought down?

Pouvez-vous faire descendre mes bagages?

P⊚-V◯-V⊚ F⒠R D◯-S⒜ñ-DR⒰
M◯ B⒜̃-G⒜ZH

Can you call a taxi for me?

Appelez-moi un taxi, s'il vous plaît.

ah-PLA MWah uhñ TAK-SEE SVP

I had a very good time!

Je me suis bien amusé!

ZHuh Muh SWEE BEE-ahñ
Nah-Mew-ZA

Thanks for everything.

Merci pour tout.

MeR-SEE PooR Too

I'll see you next time.

A la prochaine.

ah Lah PRO-SHaN

Good-bye.

Au revoir.

O Ruh-VWahR

RESTAURANT SURVIVAL

From sidewalk cafés to the most elegant restaurants, you will find a delectable assortment of French cuisine. Bon appetit!

- Breakfast, **le petit déjeuner**, is usually small and served at your hotel. Lunch, **le déjeuner**, is normally served from 12:30 PM to 3 PM. Dinner, **le dîner**, begins after 7 PM and can extend for hours. It is more formal than lunch and a time for enjoyment of great French cuisine and wine!

- You will find menus posted outside eating establishments and they may contain the following statements: **Service Compris** (service included) or **Non Compris** (service not included). Most restaurants include tax and a service charge.

- Some restaurants may charge for meals by **prix-fixe,** a set menu usually including two or three courses for one set price or **a la carte**.

- Café prices will be more expensive in high tourist areas. Prices can vary by counter or table seating.

KEY WORDS

Breakfast

le petit déjeuner

Luh Puh-TEE DA-ZHou-NA

Lunch

le déjeuner

Luh DA-ZHou-NA

Dinner

le dîner

Luh DEE-NA

Waiter

Monsieur

Muh-SYou

Waitress

Mademoiselle

MahD-MWah-ZeL

Restaurant

le restaurant

Luh ReS-TO-Rahñ

USEFUL PHRASES

A table for...
Une table à...

@N T@B-L@ @...

2	4	6
deux	quatre	six
D@	K@-TR@	S@S

The menu, please.
La carte, s'il vous plaît.

L@ K@RT SVP

Separate checks, please.
L'addition individuelle, s'il vous plaît.

L@-D@-S@-O@
@@-D@-V@-J@-@L SVP

We are in a hurry.
Nous sommes pressés.

N@ S@M PR@-S@

What do you recommend?
Qu'est-ce que vous recommandez?

K@S K@ V@ R@-K@-M@@-D@

Please bring me...

Apportez-moi... s'il vous plaît.

@h-POB-T@ MW@h... svp

Please bring us...

Apportez-nous... s'il vous plaît.

@h-POB-T@ N@... svp

I'm hungry.

J'ai faim.

ZH@ F@hñ

I'm thirsty.

J'ai soif.

ZH@ SW@F

Is service included?

Le service est compris?

L@h S@B-V@S @ KOñ-PB@

The bill, please.

L'addition, s'il vous plaît.

L@h-D@-S@-Oñ svp

PHRASEMAKER

Ordering beverages is easy and a
great way to practice your French! In many foreign
countries you may have to request ice with drinks.

Please bring me...

Apportez-moi... s'il vous plaît.

ah-P◎R-T④ MW@ah... SVP

▸ **coffee**   ▸ **tea**

du café   du thé

D@ew K@ah-F④   D@ew T④

▸ **with cream**

avec de la crème

@ah-V©êK D@uh L@ah KR©êM

▸ **with sugar**

avec du sucre

@ah-V©êK D@ew S@ew-KR@uh

▸ **with lemon**

avec du citron

@ah-V©êK D@ew S©EE-TR◎ñ

▸ **with ice**

avec de la glace

@ah-V©êK D@uh L@ah GL@âS

Soft drinks

Les sodas

LⒶ SⓄ-Dⓐⁿ

Milk

Le lait

Lⓤʰ LⒶ

Hot chocolate

Le chocolat chaud

Lⓤʰ SHⓄ-KⓄ-Lⓐʰ SHⓄ

Juice

Le jus

Lⓤʰ ZHⓔʷ

Orange juice

Le jus d'orange

Lⓤʰ ZHⓔʷ DⓄ-RⓐʰñZH

Ice water

L'eau glacée

LⓄ GLⓐ̃-SⒶ

Mineral water

L'eau minérale

LⓄ MⒺⒺ-NⒶ-RⓐʰL

AT THE BAR

Bartender

Le bar man

L**uh** B**ah**R M**ah**N

The wine list

La carte des vins

L**ah** K**ah**RT D**A** V**ã**ñ

Cocktail

Le cocktail

L**uh** K**ah**K-T**A**L

On the rocks

Aux glaçons

O GL**ã**-S**O**ñ

Straight

Sans glaçons

S**ah**ñ GL**ah**-S**O**ñ

With lemon

Avec du citron

ah-V**ẽ**K D**ew** S**EE**-TR**O**ñ

PHRASEMAKER

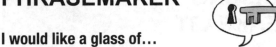

I would like a glass of…

Je voudrais un verre…

ZHuh VOO-DRA uhñ VёR…

▸ **champagne**

de champagne

Duh SHañ-Pañ-Yuh

▸ **beer**

de bière

Duh BEE-ёR

▸ **wine**

de vin

Duh Vãñ

▸ **red wine**

de vin rouge

Duh Vãñ ROOZH

▸ **white wine**

de vin blanc

Duh Vãñ BLahñ

ORDERING BREAKFAST

In France **"le petit déjeuner"** (breakfast) is usually small, consisting of a croissant or French bread with butter and jam and accompanied by café au lait, hot tea, or hot chocolate.

Bread

Le pain

L︎uh P︎ahñ

Toast

Le toast

L︎uh T︎OST

with butter

avec du beurre

ah-V︎ēK D︎ew B︎ouR

with jam

avec de la confiture

ah-V︎ēK D︎uh L︎ah K︎Oñ-F︎EE-T︎ewR

Cereal

Les céréales

L︎A S︎A-R︎A-ah︎L

PHRASEMAKER

I would like…

Je voudrais...

ZH(uh) V(oo)-DR(A)...

▶ **two eggs…**

deux oeufs...

D(ou) Z(ou)...

▶ **scrambled**

brouillés

BR(oo)-Y(A)

▶ **fried**

sur le plat

S(ew)R L(uh) PL(ah)

▶ **with bacon**

avec du bacon

(ah)-V(ē)K D(ew) B(A)-K(uh)N

▶ **with ham**

avec du jambon

(ah)-V(ē)K D(ew) ZH(ah)M-B(O)ñ

▶ **with potatoes**

avec des pommes de terre

(ah)-V(ē)K D(A) P(uh)M D(uh) T(ē)R

LUNCH AND DINNER

Although you are encouraged to sample great French cuisine, it is important to be able to order foods you are familiar with. This section will provide words and phrases to help you.

I would like…

Je voudrais...

ZH⓱ V⓪⓪-D🅡Ⓐ…

We would like…

Nous voudrions...

N⓪⓪ V⓪⓪-D🅡Ⓔ🄴-Oñ…

Bring us… please.

Apportez-nous... s'il vous plaît.

Ⓐ⓱-PⓄ🅡-TⒶ N⓪⓪… SVP

The lady would like…

La madame voudrait...

LⒶ MⒶ-DⒶM V⓪⓪-D🅡Ⓐ…

The gentleman would like…

Le monsieur voudrait...

L⓱ M⓱-SYⓄⓤ V⓪⓪-D🅡Ⓐ…

STARTERS

Appetizers

Les hors d'oeuvres

LⒶ ZⓅR-DⓇ-VRⓤ

Bread and butter

Le pain et le beurre

Lⓤ Pãñ Ⓐ Lⓤ BⓇR

Cheese

Le fromage

Lⓤ FRⓅ-MⓑZH

Fruit

Le fruit

Lⓤ FRWⓇⒺ

Salad

La salade

Lⓑ SⒶ-LⓑD

Soup

La soupe

Lⓑ SⓊP

MEATS

Bacon
Le bacon
L㉄ B㉠-K㉄N

Beef
Le boeuf
L㉄ B㉄F

Beef steak
Le bifteck
L㉄ B㉤F-T㊐K

Ham
Le jambon
L㉄ ZH㉐M-B㋒ñ

Lamb
L'agneau
L㉐-NY㋒

Pork
Le porc
L㉄ P㋒R

Veal
Le veau
L㉄ V㋒

POULTRY

Baked chicken

Le poulet au four

L@h P@@-L@ @ F@@R

Broiled chicken

Le poulet grillé

L@h P@@-L@ GR@@-Y@

Fried chicken

Le poulet frit

L@h P@@-L@ FR@@

Duck

Le canard

L@h K@-N@hR

Goose

L'oie

LW@@-@h

Turkey

La dinde

L@h D@hñD

SEAFOOD

Fish

Le poisson

Luh PWё-SOñ

Lobster

Le homard

Luh O-MahR

Oysters

Les huîtres

LA ZWEE-TRuh

Salmon

Le saumon

Luh Suh-MOñ

Shrimp

Les crevette

LA KRuh-VёT

Trout

La truite

Lah TRWEET

Tuna

Le thon

Luh TOñ

OTHER ENTREES

Sandwich
Le sandwich
Luh Sahñ-WEESH

Hot dog
Le hot-dog
Luh HahT DahG

Hamburger
Le hamburger
Luh ahM-BeR-GeR

French fries
Les frites
LA FReeT

Pasta
Les pâtes
LA PahT

Pizza
La pizza
Lah PEE-Zah

VEGETABLES

Carrots

Les carottes

LA Kah-ROT

Corn

Le maïs

Luh Mah-EES

Mushrooms

Les champignons

LA SHahñ-PEE-NYOñ

Onions

Les oignons

LA ZO-NYOñ

Potato

La pomme de terre

Lah PuhM Duh TëR

Rice

Le riz

Luh REE

Tomato

La tomate

Lah TO-MahT

FRUITS

Apple

La pomme

Lah PuhM

Banana

La banane

Lah Bah-NahN

Grapes

Les raisins

LA RA-Zãñ

Lemon

Le citron

Luh SEE-TROñ

Orange

L'orange

LO-RahñZH

Strawberry

La fraise

Lah FRěZ

Watermelon

La pastèque

Lah PahS-TěK

DESSERT

Desserts
Les desserts
L@ D@-S&B

Apple pie
La tarte aux pommes
L@ T@BT @ P@M

Cherry pie
La tarte aux cerises
L@ T@BT @ S&-B@S

Pastries
Les pâtisseries
L@ P@-T@-S&-B@

Candy
Les bonbons
L@ B@ñ B@ñ

Ice cream
La glace
L@h GL@S

Ice-cream cone
Le cône
L@h K@N

Chocolate
Au chocolat
@ SH@-K@-L@h

Strawberry
A la fraise
@h L@h FR@Z

Vanilla
A la vanille
@h L@h V@h-N@

CONDIMENTS

Butter
Le beurre
L(uh) B(ou)R

Ketchup
Le ketchup
L(uh) K(e)T-CH(uh)P

Mayonnaise
La mayonnaise
L(ah) M(A)-Y(O)-N(e)Z

Mustard
La moutarde
L(ah) M(oo)-T(ah)RD

Salt
Le sel
L(uh) S(e)L

Pepper
Le poivre
L(uh) PW(ah)-VR(uh)

Sugar
Le sucre
L(uh) S(ew)-KR(uh)

Vinegar and oil
La vinaigrette
L(ah) V(EE)-N(A)-GR(e)T

SETTINGS

A cup
Une tasse
N T@hS

A glass
Un verre
@hñ V@R

A spoon
Une cuillère
@wN KW@-@R

A fork
Une fourchette
@wN F@R-SH@T

A knife
Un couteau
@hñ K@-T@

A plate
Une assiette
@wN N@h-S@-@T

A napkin
Une serviette
@wN S@R-V@-@T

HOW DO YOU WANT IT COOKED?

Baked

Cuit au four

KW(EE)T (O) F(OO)R̰

Broiled

Grillé

GR̰(EE)-Y(A)

Steamed

A l'étuvée

(ah) L(A)-T(ew)-V(A)

Fried

Frit

FR̰(EE)

Rare

Saignant

S(A)-NY(ah)ñ

Medium

A point

(ah) PW(ah)ñ

Well done

Bien cuit

B(EE)-(ah)ñ KW(EE)

PROBLEMS

I didn't order this.

Je n'ai pas commandé ceci.

ZH⓾ N🅐 P🅐
K◎-M🅐N-D🅐 S⓾-S🅔🅔

Is the bill correct?

Il y a une erreur dans la note?

🅔🅔L 🅔🅔 🅐 🅔🅦N 🅔🅔R-R◎◎R
D🅐ñ L🅐 N◎T

Please bring me.

Apportez-moi... s'il vous plaît.

🅐-P◎R-T🅐 MW🅐... SVP

GETTING AROUND

Getting around in a foreign country can be an adventure in itself! Taxi and bus drivers do not always speak English, so it is essential to be able to give simple directions. The words and phrases in this chapter will help you get where you're going.

- The best way to get a taxi is to ask your hotel or restaurant to call one for you or go to the nearest taxi stand, **Stationnement de Taxi.** Tipping is customary.

- Trains are used frequently by visitors to Europe. They are efficient and provide connections between large cities and towns throughout the country. Arrive early to allow time for ticket purchasing and checking in, and remember, trains leave on time!

- **Le Métro** or subway is an inexpensive underground train system in Paris. It is easily accessible and a great way to get around. **"M"** signifies a metro stop!

- Check with your travel agent about special rail passes that allow unlimited travel within a set period of time.

KEY WORDS

Airport

L' aéroport

Lah-A-RO-POR

Bus Station / Bus Stop

Le gare routière
L'arrêt de bus

Luh Gah-R Roo-TEE-eR

Lah-Re Duh BewS

Car Rental Agency

L'agence de location

Lah-ZHahñS Duh LO-Kah-SEE-Oñ

Subway Station

Le métro

Luh MA-TRO

Taxi Stand

La station de taxis

Lah STah-SEE-Oñ Duh TaK-SEE

Train Station

La gare

Lah GahR

AIR TRAVEL

Arrivals	**Departures**
Les arrivées	Les départs
L@ Z@h-R©©-V@	L@ D@-P@hR

Flight number

Le vol numéro

L@h V©L N©w-M@-R©

Airline

La ligne aérienne

L@h L©©N-Y@h @h-@-R©©-©N

The gate

La porte

L@h P©RT

Information

Les renseignements

L@ R@hñ-S©N-Y@h-M@hñ

Ticket (airline)

Le billet

L@h B©©-Y@

Reservations

Les réservations

L@ R@-S©R-V@h-S©©-©ñ

PHRASEMAKER

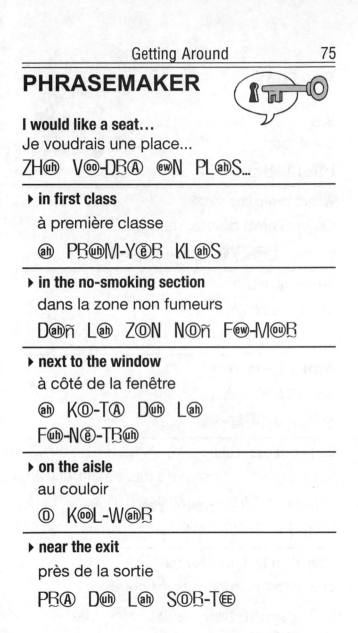

I would like a seat…
Je voudrais une place...
ZHuh Voo-DRA ewN PLahS...

▸ **in first class**
à première classe
ah PRuhM-YěR KLahS

▸ **in the no-smoking section**
dans la zone non fumeurs
Dahñ Lah ZON NOñ Few-MouR

▸ **next to the window**
à côté de la fenêtre
ah KO-TA Duh Lah
Fuh-Ně-TRuh

▸ **on the aisle**
au couloir
O Kool-WahR

▸ **near the exit**
près de la sortie
PRA Duh Lah SOR-TEE

BY BUS

Bus

L'autobus

L⊙-T⊙-B⒠S

Where is the bus stop?

Où est l'arrêt d'autobus?

⓪ Ⓐ Lⓐ-Rⓔ̆ D⊙-T⊙-B⒠

Do you go to…?

Vous allez à...?

V⊚ Z̲ⓐ-LⒶ ⓐ…

What is the fare?

C'est combien?

SⒶ K⊙ñ-Bⓔ-ⓐñ

Do I need exact change?

Est-ce que j'ai besoin de monnaie précise?

ⓔ̆S-K⒰ ZHⒶ B⒰-ZWⓐñ D⒰
M⊙-NⒶ PR̲Ⓐ-S⒠S

How often do the buses run?

Les autobus sont tous les combien?

LⒶ Z̲⊙-T⊙-B⒠S S⊙ñ T⊚ LⒶ
K⊙ñ-Bⓔ-ⓐñ

PHRASEMAKER

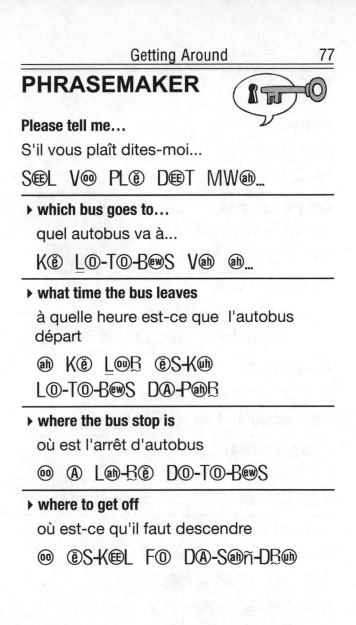

Please tell me...

S'il vous plaît dites-moi...

SᴇᴇL Vⁿ PLᴇ̃ DᴇᴇT MWₐₕ...

▸ **which bus goes to...**

quel autobus va à...

Kᴇ̃ Lⁿ-Tⁿ-BᵉʷS Vₐₕ ₐₕ...

▸ **what time the bus leaves**

à quelle heure est-ce que l'autobus départ

ₐₕ Kᴇ̃ Lⁿᵘ̃B ᴇ̃S-Kᵘʰ Lⁿ-Tⁿ-BᵉʷS Dₐₕ-PₐₕB

▸ **where the bus stop is**

où est l'arrêt d'autobus

ⁿ Ⓐ Lₐₕ-Bᴇ̃ Dⁿ-Tⁿ-BᵉʷS

▸ **where to get off**

où est-ce qu'il faut descendre

ⁿ ᴇ̃S-KᴇᴇL Fⁿ Dₐₕ-Sₐₕñ-DBᵘʰ

BY CAR

Fill it up.

Faites le plein.

F̃ēT Lⓤⓗ PLⓐⓗñ

Can you help me?

Vous pouvez m'aider?

Vⓞⓞ Pⓞⓞ-V④ M④-D④

My car won't start.

Ma voiture ne démarre pas.

Mⓐⓗ VWⓐⓗ-Tⓔⓦⓡ Nⓤⓗ D④-Mⓐⓗⓡ Pⓐⓗ

Can you fix it?

Vous pouvez la réparer?

Vⓞⓞ Pⓞⓞ-V④ Lⓐⓗ ⓡ④-Pⓐⓗ-ⓡ④

What will it cost?

Combien est-ce que cela coûte?

Kⓞñ-BⒺⒺ-ⓐⓗñ ēS-Kⓤⓗ Sⓤⓗ-Lⓐⓗ KⓞⓞT

How long will it take?

Ça va prendre combien de temps?

Sⓐⓗ Vⓐⓗ Pⓡⓐⓗñ-DⓡⓤⓗKⓞñ-BⒺⒺ-ⓐⓗñ Dⓤⓗ Tⓐⓗñ

PHRASEMAKER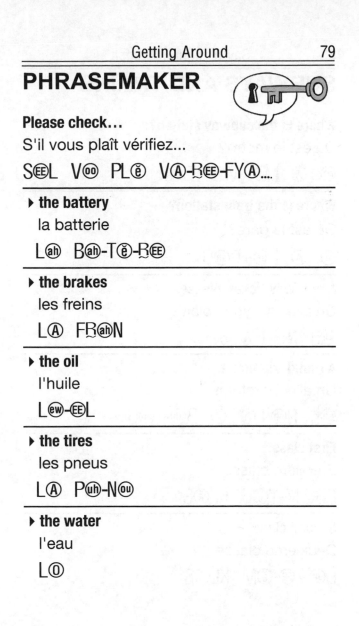

Please check…

S'il vous plaît vérifiez...

SⒺⒺL VⓄⓄ PLⓔ̃ VⒶ-ⓇⒺⒺ-FYⒶ....

▸ **the battery**

la batterie

LⒶ Bⓐⓗ-Tⓔ̃-ⓇⒺⒺ

▸ **the brakes**

les freins

LⒶ FⓇⓐⓗN

▸ **the oil**

l'huile

Lⓔ̃ⓦ-ⒺⒺL

▸ **the tires**

les pneus

LⒶ Pⓤⓗ-NⓄⓊ

▸ **the water**

l'eau

LⓄ

SUBWAYS AND TRAINS

Where is the subway station?

Où est le métro?

ⓞⓞ　Ⓐ　Lⓤⓗ　MⒶ-TRⓄ

Where is the train station?

Où est la gare?

ⓞⓞ　Ⓐ　Lⓐⓗ　GⓐⓗR

A one-way ticket, please.

Un aller, s'il vous plaît.

ⓤⓗñ　Nⓐⓗ-LⒶ　svp

A round trip ticket.

Un aller et retour.

ⓤⓗñ　Nⓐⓗ-LⒶ　Ⓐ　Rⓤⓗ-TⓄⓄR

First class

Première classe

PRⓤⓗM-YⓔR　KLⓐS

Second class

Deuxième classe

Dⓞⓤ-ZEE-ⓔM　KLⓐS

Which train do I take to go to…?

Quel train est-ce que je prends
pour aller à...?

KĕL TRãñ ĕS-Kuh ZHuh PRahñ
PooR ah-LA ah...

What is the fare?

C'est combien?

SA KOñ-BEE-ahñ

Is this seat taken?

La place est libre?

Lah PLahS A LEE-BRuh

Do I have to change trains?

Est-ce qu'il faut changer de train?

ĕS-KEEL FO SHahñ-ZHA Duh TRãñ

Does this train stop at…?

Est-ce que ce train s'arrête à...?

ĕS-Kuh Suh TRãñ Sah-Rĕ Tah...

Where are we?

Où sommes-nous?

oo SOM Noo

BY TAXI

Can you call a taxi for me?

Appelez-moi un taxi, s'il vous plaît.

ⓐ-PLⒶ MWⓐ ⓤⓗñ TⓐK-Sⓔⓔ SVP

Are you available?

Vous êtes libre?

Vⓞⓞ Ẕⓔ̃T Lⓔⓔ-BⓇⓤⓗ

I want to go…

Je voudrais aller...

ZHⓤⓗ Vⓞⓞ-DⓇⒶ ⓐ-LⒶ...

Stop here, please.

Arrêtez ici, s'il vous plaît.

ⓐ-Ⓡⓔ̃-TⒶ Ẕⓔⓔ-Sⓔⓔ SVP

Please wait.

Attendez, s'il vous plaît.

ⓐ-Tⓐñ-DⒶ SVP

How much do I owe you?

Combien est-ce que je dois?

KⓞñBⓔⓔ-ⓐñ ⓔ̃S-Kⓤⓗ ZHⓤⓗ DWⓐ

PHRASEMAKER

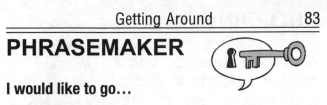

I would like to go…

Je voudrais aller...

ZH⒰ V⊚-DR⒜ Z⒜-L⒜...

▸ **to this address**

à cet adresse

⒜ SẽT ⒜-DRẽS

▸ **to the airport**

à l'aéroport

⒜ L⒜-⒜-R⊙-P⊙R

▸ **to the bank**

à la banque

⒜ L⒜ B⒜NK

▸ **to the hotel**

à l'hôtel

⒜ L⊙-TẽL

▸ **to the hospital**

à l'hôpital

⒜ L⊙-Pᴇᴇ-T⒜L

▸ **to the subway station**

au métro

⊙ M⒜-TR⊙

SHOPPING

Whether you plan a major shopping spree or just need to purchase some basic necessities, the following information is useful.

- Palais de Congrès de Paris and Forum des Halles are popular shopping centers in Paris.

- Department stores are open Monday through Saturday between 9:30 AM and 6:00 PM. Smaller stores may close for lunch between noon and 2:00 PM. Outdoor markets are only open for limited hours.

- There are three main flea markets in Paris providing wonderful opportunities to find treasures.

- Always keep receipts for everything you buy!

SIGNS TO LOOK FOR:

BOULANGERIE (Bakery)

BUREAU DE TABAC (Smoke shop, stamps)

CARTES POSTALES (Post cards)

GRAND MAGASIN (Department store)

CHAUSSURES (Shoes)

SUPERMARCHE (Supermarket)

KEY WORDS

Credit card

La carte de crédit

L@h K@hRT D@h KR@-D@@

Money

L'argent

L@hR-ZH@hñ

Receipt

Le reçu

L@h R@h-S@w

Sale

La vente

L@h V@hñT

Store

Le magasin

L@h M@-G@-Z@hñ

Travelers' checks

Les chèques de voyage

L@ SH@K D@h VW@h-Y@hZH

USEFUL PHRASES

Do you sell…?

Est-ce que vous vendez…?

ⓔS-Kⓤⓗ Vⓞⓞ Vⓐⓝ-DⒶ…

Do you have…?

Avez-vous…?

ⓐⓗ-VⒶ Vⓞⓞ…

I want to buy…

Je voudrais acheter…

ZHⓤⓗ Vⓞⓞ-DRⒶ ⓐⓗSH-TⒶ…

How much?

Combien?

KⓄⓝ-BⒺⒺ-ⓐⓗⓝ

When are the shops open?

Quand est-ce que les boutiques s'ouvrent?

Kⓐⓗⓝ TⓔS-Kⓤⓗ LⒶ
Bⓞⓞ-TⒺⒺK Sⓞⓞ-VRⓤⓗ

No, thank you.

Non, merci.

NⓄⓝ MⓔR-SⒺⒺ

I'm just looking.

Je regarde seulement.

ZH⓾ R⓾-G⓪RD S⓪L-M⓪ñ

It's very expensive.

C'est trop cher.

S⓪ TR⓪ SH⓪R

Can't you give me a discount?

Pouvez-vous me donner un prix réduit?

P⓪-V⓪ V⓪ M⓾ D⓪-N⓪ ⓾ñ
PR⓮ R⓪-DW⓮

I'll take it!

Je le prendrai!

ZH⓾ L⓾ PR⓪ñ-DR⓪

I'd like a receipt please.

Je voudrais un reçu.

ZH⓾ V⓪-DR⓪ ⓾ñ R⓾-S⓮w

I want to return this.

Je voudrais rendre ceci.

ZH⓾ V⓪-DR⓪ R⓪ñ-DR⓾ S⓾-S⓮

It doesn't fit.

Ça ne va pas.

S⓪ N⓾ V⓪ P⓪

PHRASEMAKER

I'm looking for…

Je cherche...

ZH⒰ SH⒠RSH…

▶ **a bakery**

une boulangerie

⒠N B⒪⒪-L⒜ñ-ZH⒰-R⒠⒠

▶ **a bank**

une banque

⒠N B⒜NK

▶ **a barber**

un coiffeur

⒰ñ KW⒜-F⒠R

▶ **a camera shop**

un magasin de photo

⒰ñ M⒜-G⒰-S⒜ñ D⒰ F⒪-T⒪

▶ **a hair dresser**

un coiffeur

⒰ñ KW⒜-F⒠R

▶ **a pharmacy**

une pharmacie

⒠N F⒜R-M⒜-S⒠⒠

PHRASEMAKER

Do you sell...

Est-ce que vous vendez...

ⓔS-Kⓤ Vⓞⓞ Vⓐñ-Dⓐ...

▸ **aspirin?**

l'aspirine?

LⓐS-Pⓔⓔ-RⓔⓔN

▸ **cigarettes?**

les cigarettes?

Lⓐ Sⓔⓔ-Gⓐ-RⓔT

▸ **deodorant?**

le deodorant?

Lⓤ Dⓐ-ⓞ-Dⓞ-Rⓐñ

▸ **dresses?**

les robes?

Lⓐ RⓞB

▸ **film?**

la pellicule?

Lⓐ Pⓔ-Lⓔⓔ-KⓔⓦL

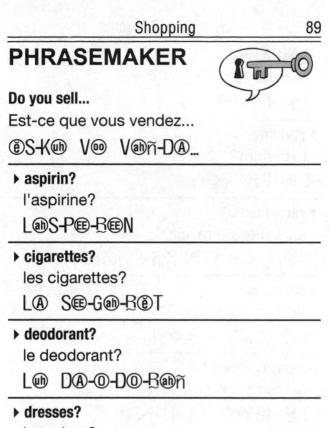

▸ **pantyhose?**
le collant?

L⑩ KⓄ-L⑩ñ

▸ **perfume?**
le parfum?

L⑩ P⑯R-F⑩ñ

▸ **razor blades?**
les lames de rasoir?

LⒶ L⑯M D⑩ Ⓡ⑯-SW⑯R

▸ **shampoo?**
le shampooing?

L⑩ SH⑯M-PⓄⓄ-ⒺN

▸ **shaving cream?**
la crème à raser?

L⑯ KⓇⓔM ⑯ Ⓡ⑯-SⒶ

▸ **shirts?**
les chemises?

LⒶ SH⑩-MⒺEZ

▸ **soap?**
le savon?

L⑩ S⑯-VⓄñ

▸ **sunglasses?**

les lunettes de soleil?

L Ⓐ Lⓔ🇼-Nⓔ̃T D🇺🇭 SⓄ-LⒶ

▸ **sunscreen?**

la crème solaire?

Lⓐ🇭 KRⓔ̃M SⓄ-Lⓔ̃R

▸ **toothbrushes?**

les brosses à dents?

LⒶ BRⓄ S̲ⓐ🇭 Dⓐ🇭ñ

▸ **toothpaste?**

le dentifrice?

L🇺🇭 Dⓐ🇭ñ-TⒺⒺ-FRⒺⒺS

▸ **water?**

l'eau nature?

LⓄ Nⓐ🇭-Tⓔ🇼R

▸ **water?** (mineral)

l'eau minérale?

LⓄ MⒺⒺ-NⒶ-Rⓐ🇭L

ESSENTIAL SERVICES

THE BANK

As a traveler in a foreign country your primary contact with banks will be to exchange money. Keep in mind that many banks close on Monday and Saturday afternoon.

- The French national currency is the Euro (formerly French franc). Bank notes are in denominations of € 500, 200, 100, 50, 20, 10 and 5. Coins are in denominations of 2 and 1 €, and 50, 20, 10, 5, 2, and 1 € cents.

- Change enough funds before leaving home to pay for tips, food, and transportation to your final destination.

- Generally, you will receive a better rate of exchange at a bank than at a Bureau de Change or at the airport.

- Current exchange rates are posted in banks and published daily in city newspapers.

- ATM machines are readily available in large cities like Paris as well as smaller towns, and credit cards are accepted.

KEY WORDS

Bank

La banque

L@h B@NK

Exchange office

Le bureau de change

L@h B@w-R@ D@h SH@ñZH

Money

L'argent

L@hR-ZH@ñ

Money order

Le mandat-poste

L@h M@ñ-D@h P@ST

Travelers' checks

Les chèques de voyage

L@ SH@K D@h VW@h-Y@hZH

USEFUL PHRASES

Where is the bank?

Où est la banque?

ⓞⓞ Ⓐ Lⓐʰ BⓐʰNK

What time does the bank open?

A quelle heure est-ce que la banque s'ouvre?

ⓐʰ Kⓔ̄ Lⓞⓤʀ ⓔ̄S-Kⓤʰ
Lⓐʰ BⓐʰNK Sⓞⓞ-VʀⓤʰＵ

Where is the exchange office?

Où est le bureau de change?

ⓞⓞ Ⓐ Lⓤʰ Bⓔʷ-ʀⓄ Dⓤʰ SHⓐʰñZH

What time does the exchange office open?

A quelle heure s'ouvre le bureau de change?

ⓐʰ Kⓔ̄ Lⓞⓤʀ Sⓞⓞ-VʀⓤʰＵ Lⓤʰ
Bⓔʷ-ʀⓄ Dⓤʰ SHⓐʰñZH

Can I change dollars here?

Puis-je changer des dollars ici?

PWⒺⒺ-ZHⓤʰ SHⓐʰñ-ZHⒶ DⒶ
DⓄ-Lⓐʰʀ ⒺⒺ-SⒺⒺ

Can you change this?

Pouvez-vous changer ceci?

P⊚-V⒜ V⊚ SH⒜ñ-ZH⒜ S⒰-S㋪

What is the exchange rate?

Quel est le taux de change?

K㋪ L⒜ L⒰ T⓪ D⒰ SH⒜ñZH

I would like large bills.

Je voudrais de grands billets.

ZH⒰ V⊚-DR⒜ D⒰
GR⒜ñ B㋪-Y⒜

I would like small bills.

Je voudrais de petits billets.

ZH⒰ V⊚-DR⒜ D⒰ P⒰-T㋪ B㋪-Y⒜

I need change.

J'ai besoin de monnaie.

ZH⒜ B⒰-ZW⒜ñ D⒰ M⓪-N⒜

Do you have an ATM?

Avez-vous un GAB?

⒜-V⒜ V⊚ ⒰ñ ZH⒜ ⒜ B⒜

POST OFFICE

PTT and **POSTE** identify the post office. Stamps can be purchased at a **Bureau de Tabac**, as well as at certain cafés and in post offices.

KEY WORDS

Airmail

Par avion

P@R @-V€-On

Letter

La lettre

L@ L€-TR@

Post office

La poste

L@ P©ST

Postcard

La carte postale

L@ K@RT P©S-T@L

Stamp

Le timbre

L@ T@ñ-BR@

USEFUL PHRASES

Where is the post office?

Où est la poste?

oo A Lah POST

What time does the post office open?

A quelle heure est-ce que la poste s'ouvre?

ah Keh Lour eS-Kuh Lah
POST Soo-VRuh

I need stamps.

J'ai besoin de timbres.

ZHA Buh-ZWahñ Duh Tahñ-BRuh

I need an envelope.

J'ai besoin d'une enveloppe.

ZHA Buh-ZWahñ DewN
ahñ-Veh-LOP

I need a pen.

J'ai besoin d'un stylo.

ZHA Buh-ZWahñ Duhñ STEE-LO

TELEPHONE

Placing phone calls in a foreign country can be a test of will and stamina! Besides the obvious language barriers, service can vary greatly from one town to the next.

- In France, phone calls can be made from the post office, Métro station, and most cafés with phone cards, **télécartes**.

- Coin operated booths still exist; however, they are often difficult to find. If you plan to make frequent use of the French phone system, it is best to purchase a **télécarte** as soon as possible.

- You can purchase a telephone card at tobacconists, post offices, and approved sales points which display the poster **TELECARTE EN VENTE ICI**. These cards allow you to easily make calls in most phone booths in France.

KEY WORDS

Information

Les renseignements

L△ R@ñ-S@N-Y@-M@ñ

Long distance

De communication interurbaine

D@ K◎-M@-N€€-K@-S€€-◎ñ

@ñ-T@R-@R-B@N

Operator

Le standardiste

L@ ST@N-D@R-D€€ST

Phone book

L'annuaire

L@-N@-@R

Public telephone

Le téléphone public

L@ T△-L△-F◎N P@-BL€€K

Telephone

Le téléphone

L@ T△-L△-F◎N

USEFUL PHRASES

May I use your telephone?

Puis-je me servir de votre téléphone?

PW☉-ZH⑩ M⑩ S☉R-V☉R D⑩
V☉-TR⑩ T☉-L☉-F☉N

Operator, I don't speak French.

Madame (f) (monsieur) (m)
le standardiste, je ne parle pas français.

M☉-D☉M (M⑩-SY☉)
L⑩ ST☉N-D☉R-D☉ST ZH⑩N-⑩
P☉RL P☉ FR☉ñ-S☉

I would like to make a long-distance call.

Je voudrais faire un appel au longue
distance.

ZH⑩ V☉-DR☉ F☉R ⑩ñ ☉-P☉L
L☉NG D☉S-T☉NS

I would like to make a call to the United States.

Je voudrais faire un appel aux Etats-Unis.

ZH⑩ V☉-DR☉ F☉R ⑩ñ ☉-P☉L
☉ Z☉-T☉ Z☉-N☉

I want to call...

Je voudrais téléphoner...

ZH⑩ V⑳-D℞Ⓐ TⒶ-LⒶ-FⓄ-NⒶ...

SIGHTSEEING AND ENTERTAINMENT

In most towns in France you will find tourist information offices. Here you can usually obtain brochures, maps, historical information, bus and train schedules.

Lively places, an abundance of atmosphere, shopping, festivals, great food, and fine wine invite travelers to experience all that France has to offer.

PARIS SIGHTS

L'Arc de Triomphe
LaRK Duh TREE-OnF

Le Louvre
Luh Loo-VRuh

La Tour Eiffel
Lah TooR EE-FeL

Notre Dame
NO-TRuh DahM

Les Champs-Elysées
LA SHahñ-ZA-LEE-ZA

KEY WORDS

Admission

L'entrée

Lⓐñ-TRⒶ

Map

Le plan

Lⓤⓗ PLⓐñ

Reservation

La réservation

Lⓐ RⒶ-SⓔⓇ-Vⓐ-SⒺⒺ-Oñ

Ticket

Le ticket

Lⓤⓗ TⒺⒺ-KⒶ

Tour

La visite

Lⓐ VⒺⒺ-ZⒺⒺT

Tour guide

Le guide

Lⓤⓗ GⒺⒺD

USEFUL PHRASES

Where is the tourist office?

Où est l'office de tourisme?

(oo) (A) LO-F(ee)S D(uh)
T(oo)R-(ee)Z-M(ah)

Is there a tour to…?

Y a-t-il une visite guidée à…?

(ee) (ah)-T(ee)L (ew)N V(ee)-Z(ee)T
G(ee)-D(A) (ah)…

Where do I buy a ticket?

Où puis-je acheter un ticket?

(oo) PW(ee)-ZH(uh) (ah)SH-T(A)
(uh)ñ T(ee)-K(A)

How much does the tour cost?

Combien coûte la visite?

K(O)ñ-B(ee)-(ah)ñ K(oo)T L(ah) V(ee)-Z(ee)T

How long does the tour take?

La visite prend combien de temps?

L(ah) V(ee)-Z(ee)T PR(ah)ñ
K(O)ñ-B(ee)-(ah)ñ D(uh) T(ah)ñ

Does the guide speak English?

Est-ce que le guide parle anglais?

ⓔS-Kⓤⓗ Lⓤⓗ GⓔⓔD PⓐⓗⓇL ⓐⓗñ-GLⓐ

Do children pay?

Les enfant paient?

Lⓐ Zⓐⓗñ-Fⓐⓗñ Pⓐ

What time does the show start?

A quelle heure commence le spectacle?

ⓐ Kⓔ LⓞⓤⓇ KⓄ-MⓐⓗñS
Lⓤⓗ SPⓔK-TⓐKL

Do I need reservations?

Il faut avoir des réservations?

ⓔⓔL FⓄ Tⓐⓗ-VWⓐⓗⓇ Dⓐ
Ⓡⓐ-SⓔⓇ-Vⓐⓗ-Sⓔⓔ-Ⓞñ

Where can we go dancing?

Où est-ce qu'on peut danser?

ⓄⓄ ⓔS KⓄñ Pⓞⓤ Dⓐⓗñ-Sⓐ

Is there a cover charge?

Est-ce que l'entrée est payante?

ⓔS-Kⓤⓗ LⓐⓗN-TⓇⓐ Pⓐ-ⓐⓗNT

PHRASEMAKER

May I invite you…

Je vous invite...

ZH⒰ V⓪ Z̲⒜ñ-V⒠T…

▸ **to a concert?**

à un concert?

⒜ ⒰ñ K⓪ñ-S⒠R̲

▸ **to dance?**

à danser?

⒜ D⒜ñ-S⒜

▸ **to dinner?**

au dîner?

⓪ D⒠-N⒜

▸ **to the movies?**

au cinéma?

⓪ S⒠-N⒜-M⒜

▸ **to the theater?**

au théâtre?

⓪ T⒜-⒜-TR̲⒰

PHRASEMAKER

Where can I find…

Où se trouve…

⓪⓪ S⓾ TR⓪⓪V…

▶ **a health club?**

un centre sportif?

⓾ñ Sⓐñ-TR⓾ SP⓪R-T⓮F

▶ **a swimming pool?**

une piscine?

⓮N P⓮-S⓮N

▶ **a tennis court?**

un terrain de tennis?

⓾ñ T⓮-Rⓐñ D⓾ T⓮-N⓮S

▶ **a golf course?**

un terrain de golf?

⓾ñ T⓮-Rⓐñ D⓾ G⓪LF

HEALTH

Hopefully you will not need medical attention on your trip. If you do, it is important to communicate basic information regarding your condition.

- Check with your insurance company before leaving home to find out if you are covered in a foreign country. You may want to purchase traveler's insurance before leaving home.

- If you take prescription medicine, carry your prescription with you. Have your prescriptions translated before you leave home.

- Take a small first-aid kit with you.

- Your embassy or consulate should be able to assist you in finding health care.

- A GREEN CROSS indicates a pharmacy, where minor treatment can be handled by the pharmacist.

- **Droguerie** is similar to a drugstore but also sells household goods and toiletries.

- {H} indicates **l'hôpital** (hospital)

KEY WORDS

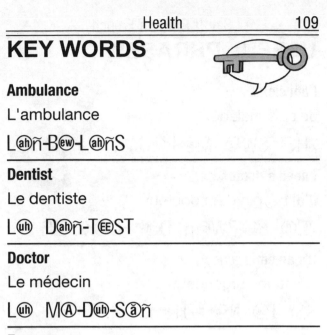

Ambulance

L'ambulance

Lⓐñ-Bⓔⱳ-LⓐñS

Dentist

Le dentiste

Lⓤ Dⓐñ-TⓔⓔST

Doctor

Le médecin

Lⓤ MⒶ-Dⓤ-Sⓐñ

Emergency

L'urgence

LⓔⱳR-ZHⓐñS

Hospital

L'hôpital

Lⓞ-Pⓔⓔ-Tⓐ L

Prescription

La prescription

Lⓐ PRⓔ-SKRⓔⓔP-Sⓔⓔ-Oñ

USEFUL PHRASES

I am sick.

Je suis malade.

ZH⒰ SW㋍ M⒜-L⒜D

I need a doctor.

J'ai besoin d'un docteur.

ZH⒜ B⒰-ZW⒜ñ D⒰ñ D⒜K-T⒪B

It's an emergency!

C'est une urgence!

S⒜ T⒠ N⒪B-ZH⒜ñS

Where is the nearest hospital?

Où est l'hôpital le plus proche?

㋏ ⒜ LO-P㋍-T⒜L
L⒰ PL⒠ PB⒜SH

Call an ambulance!

Faites venir une ambulance!

F㋑T V⒰-N㋍B ⒠ N⒜ñ-B⒠-L⒜ñS

I'm allergic to…

Je suis allergique à...

ZH⓾ SW㏳ Z̲⓪-L㊟R-ZH㏳ K̲⓪…

I'm pregnant.

Je suis enceinte.

ZH⓾ SW㏳ Z̲⓪ñ-S⓪ñT

I'm diabetic.

Je suis diabétique.

ZH⓾ SW㏳ D㏳-⓪-B㊟-T㏳K

I have a heart problem.

J'ai un problème cardiaque.

ZHⓐ ⓾N PR⓪-BL㊟M K⓪R-D㏳-⓪K

I have high blood pressure.

Je fais de l'hypertension.

ZH⓾ Fⓐ D⓾
L㏳-P㊟R-T⓪ñ-S㏳-Oñ

I have low blood pressure.

Je fais de l'hypotension.

ZH⓾ Fⓐ D⓾
L㏳-P⓪-T⓪ñ-S㏳-Oñ

PHRASEMAKER

I need...

J'ai besoin...

ZH Ⓐ Bⓤⓗ-ZWⓐⓗñ...

▶ **a doctor**

d'un docteur

Dⓤⓗñ DⓐⓗK-Tⓞⓤℝ

▶ **a dentist**

d'un dentiste

Dⓤⓗñ Dⓐⓗñ-TⒺⒺST

▶ **a nurse**

d'une infirmière

Dⓔⓦ N̲ⓐñ-FⒺⒺℝ-MⒺⒺ-ⓔℝ

▶ **an optician**

d'un opticien

Dⓤⓗñ N̲ⓄP-TⒺⒺ-SⒺⒺ-ⓐⓗñ

▶ **a pharmacist**

d'un pharmacien

Dⓤⓗñ Fⓐⓗℝ-Mⓐⓗ-SⒺⒺ-ⓐⓗñ

PHRASEMAKER

(AT THE PHARMACY)

Do you have…

Avez-vous..

@ⓗ-Vⓐ Vⓞⓞ…

▶ **aspirin?**

de l'aspirine?

Dⓤⓗ LⓐⓗS-PⒺⒺ-RⒺⒺN

▶ **Band-Aids?**

des bandages?

Dⓐ Bⓐⓗñ-DⓐⓗZH

▶ **cough medicine?**

le sirop contre la toux?

Lⓤⓗ SⒺⒺ-Rⓞ Kⓞñ-TRⓤⓗ Lⓐⓗ Tⓞⓞ

▶ **ear drops?**

les gouttes pour les oreilles?

Lⓐ GⓞⓞT PⓞⓞR Lⓐ Zⓞ-Rⓐ-Yⓞⓤ

▶ **eyedrops?**

les gouttes pour les yeux?

Lⓐ GⓞⓞT PⓞⓞR Lⓐ ZⒺⒺ-Yⓞⓤ

BUSINESS TRAVEL

It is important to show appreciation and interest in another person's language and culture, particularly when doing business. A few well-pronounced phrases can make a great impression.

I have an appointment.

J'ai rendez-vous.

ZHA RAHñ-DA-Voo

Here is my card.

Voici ma carte.

VWAH-SEE MAH KAHRT

May I speak to Mr…?

Puis-je parler à Monsieur...?

PWEE-ZHuh PAHR-LA ah Muh-SYou...

May I speak to Mrs…?

Puis-je parler à Madame...?

PWEE-ZHuh PAHR-LA ah MAH-DAHM...

I need an interpreter.

J'ai besoin d'un interprète.

ZHA Buh-ZWAñ Duhñ
NAñ-TeR-PReT

KEY WORDS

Appointment

Le rendez-vous

Luh Bahñ-DA-Voo

Meeting

La réunion

Lah BA-ewN-YOñ

Marketing

Le marketing

Luh MahB-Kё-TEEN

Presentation

La présentation

Lah PBA-SёN-Tah-SEE-Oñ

Sales

Les ventes

LA VahñT

PHRASEMAKER

I need…

J'ai besoin...

ZH④ B⑩-ZW@ñ…

▸ **a computer**

d'un ordinateur

D⑩ñ N○B-D㊰-N@-T○B

▸ **a copy machine**

d'un copieur

D⑩ñ K○-P㊰-○B

▸ **a conference room**

d'une salle de conférences

D㊰N S@L D⑩ K○ñ-F④-B@ñS

▸ **a fax machine**

d'un télécopieur

D⑩ñ T④-L④-K○-P㊰-○B

▸ **an interpreter**

d'un interprète

D⑩ñ N@ñ-T㊰B-PB㊰T

▸ **a lawyer**

d'un avocat

Duhñ Nah-VO-Kah

▸ **a notary**

d'un notaire

Duhñ NO-TëR

▸ **overnight delivery**

de livraison exprès

Duh LEE-VRA-SOñ ëKS-PRë

▸ **paper**

de papier

Duh Pah-PEE-A

▸ **a pen**

d'un stylo

Duhñ STEE-LO

▸ **a pencil**

d'un crayon

Duhñ KRA-Oñ

▸ **a secretary**

d'un secrétaire

Duhñ Së-KRë-TëR

GENERAL INFORMATION

From cool summers in the west to hot summers and very cold winters in central and eastern France, there is something for everyone!

SEASONS

Spring

Le printemps

Lⓤⓗ PRⓐñ-Tⓐⓗñ

Summer

L'été

Lⓐ-Tⓐ

Autumn

L'automne

LⓄ-Tⓤⓗñ

Winter

L'hiver

LⒺⒺ-VⓔR

THE DAYS

Monday
lundi
Luhñ-Dee

Tuesday
mardi
Mahr-Dee

Wednesday
mercredi
Mēr-KRuh-Dee

Thursday
jeudi
ZHou-Dee

Friday
vendredi
Vahñ-DRuh-Dee

Saturday
samedi
Sahm-Dee

Sunday
dimanche
Dee-MahñSH

THE MONTHS

January
janvier
ZHah̃-VEE-Ⓐ

February
février
FⒶ-VREE-Ⓐ

March
mars
MahRS

April
avril
ahV-REEL

May
mai
MⒶ

June
juin
ZHoo-ah̃

July
juillet
ZHWEE-Ⓐ

August
août
ooT

September
septembre
SⒺP-Tah̃-BRuh

October
octobre
ahK-TO-BRuh

November
novembre
NO-Vah̃-BRuh

December
décembre
DⒶ-Sah̃-BRuh

COLORS

Black

Noir (m) / Noire (f)

NW@B

White

Blanc (m) / Blanche (f)

BL@ñ / BL@ñSH

Blue

Bleu (m) / Bleue (f)

BL@

Brown

Brun (m) / Brune (f)

BR@ñ / BR@N

Gray

Gris (m) / Grise (f)

GR@ / GR@S

Gold

Or

@B

Orange

Orange

@-R@ñZH

Yellow

Jaune

ZH@N

Red

Rouge

R@ZH

Green

Vert (m) / Verte (f)

V@B / V@BT

Pink

Rose

R@Z

Purple

Violet (m) / Violette (f)

V@-@-L@ / V@-@-L@T

NUMBERS

0	1	2
Zéro	Un	Deux
ZA-RO	uhñ	Dou

3	4	5
Trois	Quatre	Cinq
TRWah	Kä-TRuh	SäNK

6	7	8
Six	Sept	Huit
SEES	SeT	WEET

9	10	11
Neuf	Dix	Onze
NouF	DEES	OñZ

12	13	14
Douze	Treize	Quatorze
DooZ	TReZ	Kä-TORZ

15	16	17
Quinze	Seize	Dix-sept
KäñZ	SeZ	DEE-SeT

18	19	
Dix-huit	Dix-neuf	
DEEZ-WEET	DEEZ-NouF	

20

Vingt

Vãn

30

Trente

TRahñT

40

Quarante

Kē-Rahñt

50

Cinquante

Sãñ-Kahñt

60

Soixante

SWah-Zahñt

70

Soixante-dix

SWah-Zahñt DēēS

80

Quatre-vingt

Kã-TRuh Vahñ

90

Quatre-vingt-dix

Kã-TRuh Vahñ DēēS

100

Cent

Sahñ

1000

Mille

MēēL

1,000,000

Million

Mēē-Lēē-Oñ

FRENCH VERBS

Verbs are the action words of any language. In French there are three main types; –**er**, –**ir**, and –**re**.

The foundation form for all verbs is called the infinitive. This is the form you will find in dictionaries. In English, we place "to" in front of the verb name to give us the infinitive; e.g., to speak. In French, **l'infinitif** is one word, **parler**, and means by itself to speak, and (as in English) it does not change its form.

On the following pages you will see the present tense conjugation of the three regular verb groups: –**er**, –**ir**, and –**re**. Conjugating a verb is what you do naturally in your own language: *I speak, he finishes, they sell*. A verb is called regular when it follows one of these three models: its basic form does not change, just the endings that correspond to the subject of the verb.

In your study of French, you will come across irregular verbs and verbs with spelling changes. Their conjugation will require memorization. However, the Phrasemaker on page 128 will help you avoid this problem. First choose a form of "want," then select an infinitive; 150 are provided in the following section. And because the infintive does not change, you don't need to worry about the conjugation of the verb or whether it is regular or irregular!

–ER VERB CONJUGATION

Find below the present tense conjugation for the regular –ER verb **parler**, meaning **to speak**. The English equivalent is: *I speak* (or *I am speaking*), *you speak* (*you are speaking*), etc. For regular –ER verbs like this, drop the infinitive ending and add **-e**, **-es**, **-e**, **-ons**, **-ez** or **-ent**.

I speak.

Je parl**e**.

ZH🔘 P🔘RL

You speak. (informal)

Tu parl**es**.

T⓪⓪ P🔘RL

He speaks. / She speaks. / (One) speaks.

Il / Elle / On parl**e**.

🔘L / 🔘L / 🔘ñ P🔘RL

We speak.

Nous parl**ons**.

N⓪⓪ P🔘R-L⓪ñ

You speak. (plural)

Vous parl**ez**.

V⓪⓪ P🔘R-L🔘

They speak.

Ils / Elles parl**ent**.

🔘L / 🔘L P🔘R-L🔘ñ

–IR VERB CONJUGATION

Find below the present tense conjugation for the regular **–IR** verb **finir**, meaning *to* finish. The English equivalent is: *I finish* (or *I am finishing*), *you finish* (*you are finishing*), etc. For regular **–IR** verbs like this, drop the infinitive ending and add **-is**, **-is**, **-it**, **-issons**, **-issez** or **-issent**.

I finish.

Je fin**is**.

ZH⓾ F⑯-N⑯

You finish. (informal)

Tu fin**is**.

T⑳ F⑯-N⑯

He finishes. / She finishes. / (One) finishes.

Il / Elle / On fin**it**.

⑯L / ⑯L / ⓐⓗñ F⑯-N⑯T

We finish.

Nous fin**issons**.

N⑳ F⑯-N⑯-S⑪ñ

You finish. (plural; formal singular)

Vous fin**issez**.

V⑳ F⑯-N⑯-Z④

They finish.

Ils / Elles fin**issent**.

⑯L / ⑯L F⑯-N⑯-Sⓐⓗñ

–RE VERB CONJUGATION

Find below the present tense conjugation for the regular **–RE** verb **vendre**, meaning *to* sell. The English equivalent is: *I sell* (or *I am selling*), *you sell* (*you are selling*), etc. For regular **–RE** verbs like this, drop the infinitive ending and add **-s**, **-s**, **-** , **-ons**, **-ez** or **-ent**.

I sell.

Je vend**s**.

ZH⓾ Vⓐ̃

You sell. (informal)

Tu vend**s**.

T⓪ Vⓐ̃

He sells. / She sells. / (One) sells.

Il / Elle / On vend.

Ⓔ L / ⓔ L / ⓐ̃ Vⓐ̃

We sell.

Nous vend**ons**.

N⓪ VⓐN-Dⓐ̃

You sell. (plural; formal singular)

Vous parl**ez**.

V⓪ Vⓐ̃-Dⓐ

They sell.

Ils / Elles vend**ent**.

Ⓔ L / ⓔ L VⓐN-Dⓐ̃

PHRASEMAKER

I want...

Je veux...

ZH⒰h V⒪⒰...

You want...

Tu veux... (informal)

T⒪⒪ V⒪⒰...

Vous voulez... (formal)

V⒪⒪ V⒪⒪-L⒜...

It is easy to recognize French verbs in their infinitive form because they always end in **-er**, **-ir**, or **-re**!

He wants... ◄

Il veut...

⒠L V⒪⒰...

► **to speak**

parl**er**

P⒜R-L⒜

She wants... ◄

Elle veut...

⒠L V⒪⒰...

► **to finish**

fin**ir**

F⒠-N⒠R

We want... ◄

Nous voulons...

N⒪⒪ V⒪⒪-L⒪ñ...

► **to sell**

vend**re**

V⒜N-DR⒰h

They want...

Ils veulent...

⒠L V⒪⒰L...

150 VERBS

Here are some essential verbs that will carry you a long way towards learning French with the EPLS Vowel Symbol System!

to add
ajouter
ⓐⓗ-ZHⓞⓞ-Tⓐ

to allow
permettre
PⓔⓡB-MⓔⓡT-TRⓤⓗ

to answer
répondre
Rⓐ-PⓞN-DRⓤⓗ

to arrive
arriver
ⓐⓗ-Rⓔⓔ-Vⓐ

to ask
demander
Dⓤⓗ-Mⓐⓗñ-Dⓐ

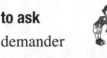

to attack
attaquer
ⓐⓗ-Tⓐⓗ-Kⓐ

to attend
assister
ⓐⓗ-SⓔⓔS-Tⓐ

to be
être
ⓔ-TRⓤⓗ

to be able
pouvoir
Pⓞⓞ-VWⓐⓗR

to beg
mendier
Mⓐⓗñ-Dⓔⓔ-ⓐ

to begin
commencer
Kⓞ-Mⓐⓗñ-Sⓐ

to bother (annoy)
embêter
ⓐⓗM-Bⓤⓗ-Tⓐ

to break
briser
BR(EE)-Z(A)

to breathe
respirer
R(ĕ)-SP(EE)-R(A)

to bring
apporter
(ah)P-P(O)R-T(A)

to build
construire
K(O)N-STR(oo)-(EE)R

to burn
brûler
BR(ou)-L(A)

to buy
acheter
(ah)SH-T(A)

to call
appeler
(ah)P-L(A)

to cancel
annuler
(ah)N-Y(oo)-L(A)

to change
changer
SH(ah)ñ-ZH(A)

to chew
mâcher
M(ă)-SH(A)

to clean
nettoyer
N(ĕ)T-TW(ah)-Y(A)

to climb
monter
M(O)N-T(A)

to close
fermer
F(ĕ)R-M(A)

to come
venir
V(uh)-N(EE)R

to cook
cuisiner
KW㽼-Z㽼-N㽼

to contact
contacter
K㎝N-T㽼K-T㽼

to count
compter
K㎝MP-T㽼

to cry
pleurer
PL㎝-R㽼

to cut
couper
K㎝-P㽼

to dance
danser
D㽼ñ-S㽼

to decide
décider
D㽼-S㽼-D㽼

to declare
déclarer
D㽼-KL㽼-R㽼

to depart
partir
P㽼R-T㽼R

disturb
déranger
D㽼-R㽼ñ-ZH㽼

to do
faire
F㽼R

to drink
boire
BW㽼R

to dry
sécher
S㽼-SH㽼

to earn
gagner
G㽼N-Y㽼

to eat

manger

M@ñ-ZH@

to enjoy

aimer

@-M@

to enter

entrer

@ñ-TR@

to entertain

divertir

D©-V®r-T©R

to envy

envier

@ñ-V©-@

to explain

expliquer

©KS-PL©-K@

to feel

sentir

S@ñ-T©R

to fight

lutter

L©T-T@

to fill

remplir

R@M-PL©R

to find

trouver

TR©-V@

to finish

finir

F©-N©R

to fix

fixer

F©K-S@

to flirt

flirter

FL©R-T@

to fly

voler

V©-L@

to forget
oublier
OOB-LEE-A

to have
avoir
AHV-WAHR

to forgive
pardonner
PAHR-DON-NA

to hear
entendre
AHÑ-TAHÑ-DRUH

to get
obtenir
OB-TĔ-NEER

to help
aider
A-DA

to give
donner
DON-NA

to hide
cacher
KAH-SHA

to go
aller
AH-LA

to hold
tenir
TĔ-NEER

to greet
saluer
SÃL-OO-A

to imagine
imaginer
EE-MAH-ZHEE-NA

to happen
se passer
SĔ PAHS-SA

to inhale
aspirer
AHS-PEE-RA

to judge

juger

ZH◎◎-ZH◉

to jump

sauter

S◎-T◉

to kiss

embrasser

◉ñ-BR◉-S◉

to know (knowledge)

savoir

S◉-VW◉R

to know (person)

connaître

K◎-N◉-TR◉

to laugh

rire

R◉-R◉

to learn

apprendre

◉P-PR◉ñ-DR◉

to leave

quitter

K◉T-T◉

to lie (not the truth)

mentir

M◉ñ-T◉R

to lift

lever

L◎◎-V◉

to listen

écouter

◉-K◎◎-T◉

to live

vivre

V◉-VR◉

to look

regarder

R◉-G◉R-D◉

to lose

perdre

P◉R-DR◉

to love
aimer
Ⓐ-MⓄ

to make
faire
FⒺR

to marry
marier
Mⓐ-RⒺ-Ⓐ

to measure
mesurer
Mⓔ-Zⓞᵘ-RⒶ

to miss
manquer
Mⓐñ-KⓐⒶ

to move
déplacer
DⒶ-PLⓐ-SⒶ

to need (require)
nécessiter
NⓔⒸ-SⓔⒺ-SⒺ-TⒶ

to notify
aviser
ⓐ-VⒺ-ZⒶ

to offer
offrir
ⓄF-FRⒺR

to open
ouvrir
ⓞⓞ-VRⒺR

to order
commander
KⓄ-MⓐN-DⒶ

to pack
emballer
ⓐM-BⓐL-LⒶ

to paint
peindre
Pⓐñ-DRⓤ

to pass
passer
PⓐS-SⒶ

to pay (for)
payer
P@-Y@

to play
jouer
ZH@-@

to pretend
prétendre
PR@-T@ñ-DR@

to print
imprimer
@M-PR@-M@

to promise
promettre
PR@-M@T-TR@

to pronounce
prononcer
PR@-N@N-S@

to push
pousser
P@S-S@

to put
mettre
M@T-TR@

to quit
quitter
K@-T@

to read
lire
L@-R@

to recomend
recommander
R@-K@-M@ñ-D@

to rent
louer
L@-@

to remember
rappeler
R@-PL@

to rescue
sauver
S@-V@

to rest	**to show**
reposer	montrer
Ruh-PO-ZA	MOñ-TRA
to return	**to sign**
retourner	signer
Ruh-TOR-NA	SEEN-YA
to run	**to sing**
courir	chanter
KOO-REER	SHahñ-TA
to say	**to sit**
dire	s'asseoir
DEE-Ruh	Suh-SWahR
to see	**to sleep**
voir	dormir
VWahR	DOR-MEER
to sell	**to smoke**
vendre	fumer
Vahñ-DRuh	Few-MA
to send	**to smile**
envoyer	sourire
ahN-Voy-YA	Soo-REE-Ruh

to speak

parler

P@B-L@

to spell

épeler

@-PL@

to spend (money)

dépenser

D@-P@ñ-S@

to start (begin)

commencer

K@-M@ñ-S@

to stay

rester

R@-ST@

to stop

arrêter

@-R@-T@

to study

étudier

@-T@-D@-@

to swim

nager

N@-ZH@

to take

prendre

PR@ñ-DR@

to talk

parler

P@B-L@

to teach

enseigner

@ñ-S@N-Y@

to tell

raconter

R@-K@ñ-T@

to touch

toucher

T@-SH@

to think

penser

P@ñ-S@

to travel

voyager

VW@h-Y@h-ZH@

to try

essayer

@S-S@-Y@

to understand

comprendre

K@M-PR@hñ-DR@

to use

utiliser

@-T@-L@-Z@

to visit

visiter

V@-Z@-T@

to wait

attendre

@T-T@hñ-DR@

to walk

marcher

M@R-SH@

to want

vouloir

V@L-W@hR

to wash

laver

L@h-V@

to watch

regarder

R@-G@hR-D@

to win

gagner

G@hN-Y@

to work

travailler

TR@h-V@-Y@

to worry

inquiéter

@hñ-K@-T@

to write

écrire

@-KR@-R@

DICTIONARY

Each English entry is followed
by the French word and then
the EPLS Vowel Symbol System.
French nouns are either masculine
or feminine. The French article

le precedes masculine nouns and **la** precedes
feminine nouns in the singular form. **Les** indicates
feminine or masculine plural. In some cases,
masculine and feminine are indicated by (m) and
(f) respectively.

A

a / an un (m) ⓤñ une (f) ⓔwN

a lot beaucoup BⓄ-Kⓞⓞ

able (to be) pouvoir Pⓞⓞ-VWⓐⒽB

above au dessus (de) Ⓞ DⓤⒽ-Sⓔw (DⓤⒽ)

accident l'accident (m) LⓐⒽK-SⒺⒺ-DⓐⒽñ

accommodation le logement LⓤⒽ LⓄZH-MⓐⒽñ

account le compte LⓤⒽ KⓄñT

address l'adresse (f) LⓐⒽ-DBⒺS

admission l'entrée (f) LⓐⒽñ-TBⒶ

afraid (to be) avoir peur ⓐⒽ-VWⓐⒽB PⓞⒷ

after après ⓐⒽ-PBⒶ

afternoon l'après-midi (m) LⓐⒽ-PBⒶ MⒺⒺ-DⒺⒺ

air conditioning d'air climatisé (m)

    DⒺR KLⒺⒺ-Mⓐⓗ-TⒺⒺ-ZⒶ

aircraft l'avion (m) Lⓐⓗ-VⒺⒺ-Oñ

airline la ligne aérienne Lⓐⓗ LⒺⒺN ⓐⓗ-Ⓐ-RⒺⒺ-ⓔN

airport l'aéroport (m) Lⓐⓗ-Ⓐ-RⓄ-PⓄR

aisle couloir KⓄⓄL-WⓐⓗR

all tout (m) TⓄⓄ   toute (f) TⓄⓄT

almost presque PRⒺS-Kⓤⓗ

alone seul SⓄⓤL

also aussi Ⓞ-SⒺⒺ

always toujours TⓄⓄ-ZHⓄⓄR

ambulance l'ambulance (f) Lⓐⓗñ-BⒺⓦ-LⓐⓗñS

American américain (m) ⓐⓗ-MⒶ-RⒺⒺ-KⒶñ

    américaine (f) ⓐⓗ-MⒶ-RⒺⒺ-KⒺñ

and et Ⓐ

another un autre ⓤⓗñ NⓄ-TRⓤⓗ

anything quelque chose KⒺL-Kⓤⓗ SHⓄZ

apartment l'appartement (m)

    Lⓐⓗ-PⓐⓗR-Tⓤⓗ-Mⓐⓗñ

appetizers les hors-d'oeuvres (m/pl)

    LⒶ ZⓄR-DⓄⓤ-VRⓤⓗ

apple la pomme Lⓐⓗ PⓤⓗM

appointment le rendez-vous L◍ B◍ñ-D◍-V◍◍

April avril ◍-VB◍L

arrival l'arrivée (f) L◍-B◍-V◍

arrive (to) arriver ◍-B◍-V◍

ashtray le cendrier L◍ S◍ñ-DB◍-◍

aspirin l'aspirine (f) L◍S-P◍-B◍N

attention l'attention (f) L◍-T◍ñ-S◍-◍ñ

August août ◍◍T

Australia l'Australie (f) L◍-STB◍-L◍

Australian l' australien (m) L◍-STB◍-L◍◍ñ

l'australienne (f) L◍-STB◍-L◍◍ñ

author l'auteur (m) L◍-T◍B

automobile l'automobile (f) L◍-T◍-M◍-B◍L

autumn l'automne L◍-T◍ñ

avenue l'avenue L◍-V◍-N◍

awful affreux (m) ◍-FB◍

affreuse (f) ◍-FB◍Z

B

baby le bébé L◍ B◍-B◍

babysitter le garde-bébé L◍ G◍BD B◍-B◍

bacon le bacon Lⓤⓗ BⒶ-KⓤⓗN

bad mauvais (m) MⓄ-VⒶ mauvaise (f) MⓄ-Vⓔ̂Z

bag le sac Lⓤⓗ SⓐⓗK

baggage les bagages (m) LⒶ Bⓐⓗ-GⓐⓗZH

baked au four Ⓞ FⓞⓞB

bakery la boulangerie Lⓐⓗ Bⓞⓞ-Lⓐⓗñ-ZHⓤⓗ-RⓔⒺ

banana la banane Lⓐⓗ Bⓐⓗ-NⓐⓗN

bandage le bandage Lⓤⓗ BⓐⓗN-DⓐⓗZH

bank la banque Lⓐⓗ BⓐⓗñK

barbershop le salon de coiffure

Lⓤⓗ Sⓐ̂-LON Dⓤⓗ KWⓔ̂-FⓔⓦB

bartender le barman Lⓤⓗ BⓐⓗB MⓐⓗN

bath la bain Lⓐⓗ Bⓐ̂ñ

bathing suit le maillot de bains

Lⓤⓗ Mⓐⓗ-YⓄ Dⓤⓗ Bⓐ̂ñ

bathroom la salle de bains

Lⓐⓗ SⓐⓗL Dⓤⓗ Bⓐ̂ñ

battery la batterie Lⓤⓗ Bⓐⓗ-Tⓤⓗ-RⓔⒺ

beach la plage Lⓐⓗ PLⓐⓗZH

beautiful beau (m) BⓄ / belle (f) Bⓔ̂L

beauty shop le salon de beauté

Lⓤⓗ Sⓐ̂-LOñ Dⓤⓗ Bⓞⓞ-TⒶ

bed le lit L(uh) L(ee)

beef le boeuf L(uh) B(ou)F

beer la bière L(ah) B(ee)-(e)R

bellman le chasseur L(uh) SH(ah)-S(ou)R

belt la ceinture L(ah) S(a)ñ-T(ou)R

big grand (m) GR(ah)ñ

    grande (f) GR(ah)ND

bill l'addition (f) L(ah)-D(ee)-S(ee)-(O)ñ

black noir NW(ah)R

blanket la couverture L(ah) K(oo)-V(e)R-T(ou)R

blue bleu BL(ou)

boat le bateau L(uh) B(ah)-T(O)

book le livre L(uh) L(ee)-VR(uh)

bookstore la librairie L(ah) L(ee)-BR(e)-R(ee)

border la frontière L(ah) FR(O)ñ-T(ee)-(e)R

boy le garçon L(uh) G(ah)R-S(O)ñ

bracelet le bracelet L(uh) BR(ah)-S(uh)-L(A)

brake le frein L(uh) FR(ah)ñ

bread le pain L(uh) P(ah)ñ

breakfast le petit déjeuner

    L(uh) P(uh)-T(ee) D(A)-ZH(ou)-N(A)

broiled grillé (f) GR(ee)-Y(A)

brother le frère Luh FREHR

brush la brosse Lah BROS

building le bâtiment Luh Bah-TEE-MahÑ

bus l'autobus (m) LO-TO-BewS

bus station la gare routière

Lah GahR ROO-TEE-ÊR

bus stop l'arrêt de bus (m) Lah-RÊ Duh BewS

business les affaires (f) LA Zah-FÊR

butter le beurre Luh BooR

buy (to) acheter ahSH-TA

C

cab le taxi Luh TahK-SEE

call (to) appeler ah-Puh-LA

camera l'appareil-photo (m)

Lah-Pah-RA FO-TO

Canada Canada Kah-Nah-Dah

Canadian Canadien (m) KahN-ah-DEEahÑ

Canadienne (f) KahN-ah-DEEÊÑ

candy le bonbon Luh BOÑ-BOÑ

car la voiture Lah VWah-TewR

carrot la carotte Lah Kah-ROT

castle le château Luh SHah-TO

cathedral la cathédrale L🅐 K🅐-T🅐-DR🅐L

celebration la fête L🅐 FⒺT

center le centre L🅤 S🅐ñ-TR🅤

cereal les céréales L🅐 S🅐-R🅐-🅐L

chair la chaise L🅐 SHⒺZ

champagne la champagne

    L🅐 SH🅐ñ-P🅐N-Y🅤

change (to) changer SH🅐ñ-ZH🅐

change (exact) la monnaie précise

    L🅐 MⓄ-N🅐 PR🅐-SⒺS

change (money) la monnaie L🅐 MⓄ-N🅐

cheap bon marché BⓄñ M🅐B-SH🅐

check (bill in a restaurant) l'addition (f)

    L🅐-DⒺ-SⒺ-Ⓞñ

cheers à votre santé 🅐-VⓄ-TR🅤 S🅐ñ-T🅐

cheese le fromage L🅤 FRⓄ-M🅐ZH

chicken le poulet L🅤 P∞-L🅐

child l'enfant L🅐ñ-F🅐ñ

chocolate (flavor) au chocolat Ⓞ SHⓄ-KⓄ-L🅐

church l'église (f) L🅐-GLⒺZ

cigar le cigare L🅤 SⒺ-G🅐R

cigarette la cigarette L🅐 SⒺ-G🅐-RⒺT

city la ville L㋐ V㋑L

clean propre PR㋔-PR㋒

close (to) fermer F㋑R-M㋐

closed fermé F㋑R-M㋐

clothes les vêtements (m) L㋐ V㋑T-M㋐ñ

cocktail le cocktail L㋒ K㋐K-T㋐L

coffee le café L㋒ K㋐-F㋐

cold froid (m) FRW㋐ froide (f) FRW㋐D

comb le peigne L㋒ P㋑-NY㋒

come (to) venir V㋒-N㋑R

company (business) la compagnie
     L㋐ K㋔ñ-P㋐-NY㋑

computer l'ordinateur L㋔R-D㋑-N㋐-T㋒R

concert le concert L㋒ K㋔ñ-S㋑R

condom le préservatif
     L㋒ PR㋐-Z㋑R-V㋐-T㋑F

conference la conférence
     L㋐ K㋔ñ-F㋐-R㋐ñS

conference room la sale de conférences
     L㋐ S㋐L D㋒ K㋔ñ-F㋐-R㋐ñS

congratulations félicitations
     F㋐-L㋑-S㋑-T㋐-S㋑-㋔ñ

copy machine le copieur L⓪h KO-PEE-⓪⓪R

corn le maïs L⓪h M⓪h-EES

cough syrup le sirop contre la toux

　　L⓪h SEE-RO KON-TR⓪h L⓪h TOO

cover charge le couvert L⓪h KOO-V⓪R

crab le crabe L⓪h KR⓪hB

cream la crème L⓪h KR⓪M

credit card la carte de crédit

　　L⓪h K⓪hRT D⓪h KR⓪-DEE

cup la tasse L⓪h T⓪hS

customs la douane L⓪h DW⓪hN

D

dance (to) danser D⓪hñ-S⓪

dangerous dangereux (m) D⓪hñ-ZH⓪h-R⓪ou

　　dangereuse (f) D⓪hñ-ZH⓪h-R⓪ouS

date (calendar) la date L⓪h D⓪hT

day le jour L⓪h ZH⓪⓪R

December décembre D⓪-S⓪hñ-BR⓪h

delicious délicieux (m) D⓪-LEE-SEE-⓪ou

　　délicieuse (f) D⓪-LEE-SEE-⓪ouS

delighted enchanté ⓪hñ-SH⓪hñ-T⓪

dentist le dentiste L⓪h D⓪hñ-TEEST

deodorant le déodorant Luh DA-O-DO-Rahn

department store le grand magasin

Luh GRahn Mah-Gah-Zän

departure le départ Luh DA-PahR

dessert le dessert Luh DA-SёR

detour le détour Luh DA-TooR

diabetic diabétique DEE-ah-BA-TEEK

diarrhea la diarrhée Lah DEE-ah-RA

dictionary le dictionnaire Luh DEEK-SEE-O-NёR

dinner le dîner Luh DEE-NA

dining room la salle à manger

Lah SahL ah Mahn-ZHA

direction la direction Lah DEE-RёK-SEE-On

dirty sale SahL

disabled handicapé Hahn-DEE-Kah-PA

discount la remise Lah Ruh-MEEZ

distance la distance Lah DEES-Tahns

doctor le docteur Luh DahK-TooR

documents les documents (m)

LA DO-Kew-Mahn

dollar le dollar Luh DO-LahR

down descendre DёA-Sahn-DRuh

downtown en ville ⓐñ VⓔⓔL

dress la robe Lⓐ Ⓡ◎B

drink (to) boire BWⓐⓡ

drive (to) conduire K◎ñ-DWⓔⓔⓡ

drugstore la pharmacie Lⓐ Fⓐⓡ-Mⓐ-Sⓔⓔ

dry cleaner la teinturerie Lⓐ Tⓐñ-Tⓔⓦ-ⓔ-ⓡⓔⓔ

duck le canard Lⓤ Kⓐ-Nⓐⓡ

E

ear l'oreille L◎-ⓡⓐ-Yⓞⓤ

ear drops les gouttes pour les oreilles (f)

    Lⓐ G◎◎T P◎◎ⓡ Lⓐ Z◎-ⓡⓐ-Yⓞⓤ

early tôt T◎

east l'est (m) Lⓔ̃ST

easy facile Fⓐ-SⓔⓔL

eat (to) manger Mⓐñ-ZHⓐ

eggs l'oeuf L◎ⓤF

eggs (fried) les oeufs sur le plat (m/pl)

    Lⓐ z◎ⓤF Sⓔⓦⓡ Lⓤ PLⓐ

eggs (scrambled) les oeufs brouillés (m/pl)

    Lⓐ z◎ⓤF Bⓡⓔⓔ-Yⓐ

electricity l'électricité (f)

    LA-LĔK-TREE-SEE-TA

elevator l'ascenseur (m) Lah-Sahñ-SOOR

embassy l'ambassade (f) Lahñ-Bah-SahD

emergency l'urgence (f) LOOR-ZHahñS

England l'Angleterre LahNG-Luh-TĔR

English anglais (m) ahñ-GLA

    anglaise (f) ahñ-GLĔZ

enough! c'est assez! SA Tah-SA

entrance l'entrée (f) Lahñ-TRA

envelope l'enveloppe (f) Lahñ-Vuh-LOP

evening la soirée Lah SWah-RA

everything tout TOO

excellent excéllent (m) ĔK-SA-Lahñ

    excéllente (f) ĔK-SA-LahñT

excuse me pardon PahR-DOñ

exit la sortie Lah SOR-TEE

expensive cher SHĔR

eyes les yeux (m) LA ZEE-YOO

eyedrops les gouttes pour les yeux

    LA GOOT POOR LA ZEE-YOO

F

face le visage L⑩ V㉤-S⑩ZH

far loin LW⑳ñ

fare (cost) le tarif L⑩ T⑩-R㉤F

fast rapide R⑩-P㉤D

fax le fax L⑩ F⑩KS

fax machine le télécopieur
L⑩ T⑪-L⑪-K⓪-P㉤-⑩R

February février F⑪-VR㉤-⑪

few peu de P⑳ D⑩

film (camera) la pellicule L⑩ P㉤-L㉤-K⑳L

film (movie) le cinéma L⑩ S㉤-N⑪-M⑩

fine (very well) très bien TR⑪ B㉤-⑪ñ

finger le doigt L⑩ DW⑩

fire! le feu! L⑩ F⑳

fire extinguisher l'extincteur (m)
L㉤K-ST⑳ñK-T⑳R

first premier (m) PR㉤M-Y⑪
première (f) PR㉤M-Y⑪R

fish le poisson L⑩ PW⑩-S⓪ñ

flight le vol L⑩ V⓪L

florist shop le fleuriste L⑩ FL⑳-R㉤ST

flowers les fleurs L④ FL◎B

food la nourriture L⑨ N◎-B⑫-T◎B

foot le pied L⑩ PY④

fork la fourchette L⑨ F◎B-SH⑧T

France la France L⑨ FB⑨ñS

French français (m) FB⑨ñ-S④

française (f) FB⑨ñ-S⑧Z

French (language) le français L⑩ FB⑨ñ-S④

french fries les frites L④ FB⑫T

fresh frais FB④

Friday vendredi V⑨ñ-DB⑩-D⑫

fried frit (m) FB⑫   frite (f) FB⑫T

friend l'ami (m) L⑨-M⑫   l'amie (f) L⑨-M⑫

fruit le fruit L⑩ FBW⑫

funny drôle DB◎L

G

gas station la station de service

L⑨ ST⑨-S⑫-O ñ D⑩ S⑧B-V⑫S

gasoline l'essence (f) L⑧-S⑨ñS

gate la barrière L⑨ B⑨B-⑫-⑧B

gentleman monsieur M⑩-SY◎

gift le cadeau L⑩ K⑨-D◎

girl la fille L@h F©©

glass (drinking) le verre L@h V©B

glasses (eye) les lunettes L@ L©-N©T

gloves les gants L@ G@hñ

gold l'or L©B

golf le golf L@h G©LF

golf course le terrain de golf

    L@h T©-B@ñ D© G©LF

good bon (m) B©ñ bonne (f) B@hN

good-bye au revoir ©-B@h-VW@hB

grapes les raisins L@ B@-Z@ñ

grateful reconnaissant B@h-K©-N©-S@ñ

gray gris (m) GB©© grise (f) GB©©S

green vert (m) V©B verte (f) V©BT

grocery store l'épicerie (f) L@-P©-S©-B©©

group le groupe L@h GB©©P

guide le guide L@h G©©D

H

hair les cheveux (m/pl) L@ SH@h-V©

hairbrush la brosse à cheveux

    L@h BB©S @h SH@h-V©

haircut la coupe de cheveux

    Lah KooP Duh SHuh-Vou

ham le jambon Luh ZHahñ-BOñ

hamburger le hamburger

    Luh ahM-BêR-GêR

hand la main Lah Mãñ

happy heureux (m) ou-Rou

    heureuse (f) ou-RouS

have (I) J'ai ZHA

he il EEL

head la tête Lah TêT

headache mal à la tête Mah Lah Lah TêT

health club le centre sportif

    Luh Sahñ-TRuh SPOR-TEEF

heart le coeur Luh KouR

heart condition mal au coeur Mah LO-KouR

heat la chaleur Lah SHah-LouR

hello bonjour BOñ-ZHooR

help au secours O Suh-KooR

here ici EE-SEE

holiday la fête Lah FêT

hospital l'hôpital (m) LO-PEE-TahL

hot dog le hot dog L◍ H◍T D◍G

hotel l'hôtel (m) L◍-TⓔL

hour l'heure L◍R

how comment K◍-M◍ñ

hurry! dépêchez-vous! D◍-Pⓔ-SH◍ V◍◍

husband le marie (m) L◍ M◍-Rⓔⓔ

I

I je ZH◍

ice la glace L◍ GL◍S

ice cream la glace L◍ GL◍S

ice cubes le glaçons (f) L◍ GL◍-S◍ñ

ill malade M◍-L◍D

important important (m) ◍ñ-P◍B-T◍ñ

  importante (f) ◍ñ-P◍B-T◍ñT

indigestion la dyspepsie L◍ DⓔⓔS-Pⓔ̃P-Sⓔⓔ

information les renseignements (m/pl)

  L◍ R◍ñ-Sⓔ̃N-Y◍-M◍ñ

inn l'auberge (f) L◍-Bⓔ̃RZH

interpreter l'interprète (m) L◍ñ-Tⓔ̃B-PRⓔ̃T

J

jacket le veston L◍ Vⓔ̃S-T◍ñ

jam la confiture L◍ K◍ñ-Fⓔⓔ-T◍◍B

January janvier ZHahñ-VEE-A

jewelry les bijoux (m) LA BEE-ZHoo

jewelry store la bijouterie Lah BEE-ZHoo-Tē-REE

job le travail Luh TRah-Vah-You

juice le jus Luh ZHoo

June juin ZHoo-äñ

July juillet ZHoo-EE-A

K

ketchup le ketchup Luh Kē-CHuhP

key la clé Lah KLA

kiss le baiser Luh BA-SA

knife le couteau Luh Koo-TO

know (I) Je sais ZHuh SA

L

ladies' restroom Dames DahM

lady la dame Lah DahM

lamb l'agneau Lahñ-YO

language la langue Lah LahNG

large grand (m) GRahñ grande (f) GRahND

late tard TahR

laundry la blanchisserie   Luh BLahñ-SHEE-Suh-Ree

lawyer l'avocat (m)   Lah-VO-Kah

left (direction) à gauche (f)   ah GOSH

leg la jambe   Luh ZHahñB

lemon le citron   Luh SEE-TROñ

less moins   MWAñ

letter la lettre   Lah Leh-TRuh

lettuce la laitue   Lah LA-Tew

light la lumière   Lah LewM-Yehr

like comme   KOM

like (I)   Je veux   ZHuh Voo

like (I would)   Je voudrais   ZHuh Voo-DRA

lip la lèvre   Lah Leh-VRuh

lipstick le rouge   Luh ROOZH

little petit (m)   Puh-TEE   petite (f)   Puh-TEET

live (to) vivre   VEE-VRuh

lobster le homard   Luh O-Mahr

long long (m)   LOñ   longue (f)   LONG

lost perdu   Pehr-Dew

love l'amour   Lah-MooR

luck la chance   Lah SHahñS

luggage les bagages (m) L④ B⑤-G⑥ZH

lunch le déjeuner L⑩ D④-ZH⑩-N④

M

maid la domestique L⑥ D⑥M-⑥S-T⑥K

mail le courrier L⑩ K⑩-R⑥-④

makeup le maquillage L⑩ M⑥-K⑥-Y⑥ZH

man l'homme (m) L⑥M

manager le gérant L⑩ ZH④-R⑥ñ

map le plan L⑩ PL⑥ñ

March mars M⑥RS

market le marché L⑩ M⑥R-SH④

match (light) l'allumette (f) L⑥-L⑥w-M⑥T

May mai M④

mayonnaise la mayonnaise L⑥ M⑥-Y⑥-N⑥Z

meal le repas L⑩ R⑩-P⑥

meat la viande L⑥ V⑥-⑥ñD

mechanic le mécanicien

L⑩ M④-K⑥-N⑥-S⑥-⑥ñ

medicine le médecine L⑩ M④-D⑩-S⑥N

meeting le rendez-vous L⑩ R⑥ñ-D④-V⑩

mens' restroom messieurs M⑥-SY⑩

menu la carte L⑥ K⑥RT

message le message L⬤ M⬤-S⬤-ZH

milk le lait L⬤ L⬤

mineral water l'eau minérale (f)

  L⬤ M⬤-N⬤-R⬤L

minute le minute L⬤ M⬤-N⬤T

Miss mademoiselle M⬤D-MW⬤-Z⬤L

mistake la faute L⬤ F⬤T

misunderstanding le malentendu

  L⬤ M⬤L-⬤ñ-T⬤ñ-D⬤

moment le moment L⬤ M⬤-M⬤ñ

Monday lundi L⬤ñ-D⬤

money l'argent (m) L⬤R-ZH⬤ñ

month le mois L⬤ MW⬤

monument le monument L⬤ M⬤-N⬤-M⬤ñ

more plus PL⬤

morning le matin L⬤ M⬤-T⬤ñ

mosque la mosquée L⬤ M⬤S-K⬤

mother la mère L⬤ M⬤R

mountain la montagne L⬤ M⬤ñ-T⬤N-Y⬤

movie le cinéma L⬤ S⬤-N⬤-M⬤

Mr. monsieur M⬤-SY⬤

Mrs. madame M⬤-D⬤M

much (too) trop TRO

museum le musée Luh Mew-ZA

mushroom le champignon

   Luh SHahñ-PEEN-YON

music la musique Lah Mew-ZEEK

mustard la moutarde Lah MOO-TahRD

N

nail polish la vernis à ongles

   Lah VēR-NEE Sah Oñ-GLuh

name le nom Luh NOñ

napkin la serviette Lah SēR-VEE-ēT

near près de PRA Duh

neck le cou Luh Koo

need (I) J'ai besoin ZHA Buh-ZWañ

never jamais ZHah-MA

newspaper le journal Luh ZHOOR-NahL

news stand le kiosque Luh KEE-ahSK

night la nuit Lah NWEE

nightclub la boite de nuit

   Lah BWahT Duh NWEE

no non NOñ

no smoking non fumeurs NOñ Few-MOOR

noon midi M(EE)-D(EE)

north le nord L(uh) NⓄR̰

notary le notaire L(uh) NⓄ-T(ĕ)R̰

November novembre NⓄ-V(ah)ñ-BR̰(uh)

now maintenant M(ă)ñ-T(uh)-N(ah)ñ

number le numéro L(uh) N(ew)-MⒶ-R̰Ⓞ

nurse l'infirmière (f) L(ă)ñ-F(EE)R̰-M(EE)-(ĕ)R̰

O

occupied occupé Ⓞ-K(ew)-PⒶ

ocean l'océan (m) LⓄ-SⒶ-(ah)ñ

October octobre ⓄK-TⓄ-BR̰(uh)

officer l'officier (m) LⓄ-F(EE)-S(EE)-Ⓐ

oil l'huile (f) L(ew)-(EE)L

omelet l'omelette (f) LⓄM-L(ĕ)T

one way (traffic) sens unique S(ah)ñS (ew)-N(EE)K

onions les oignons LⒶ Z̲Ⓞ-NYⓄñ

open (to) ouvrir (oo)-VR̰(EE)R̰

opera l'opéra (m) LⓄ-PⒶ-R̰(ah)

operator le standardiste L(uh) ST(ah)N-D(ah)R̰-D(EE)ST

optician l'opticien LⓄP-T(EE)-S(EE)-(ah)ñ

orange (color) orange O-RahÑ-ZH

orange (fruit) l'orange (f) LO-RahÑZH

order (to) commander KO-MahÑ-DA

original original O-REE-ZHEE-NahL

owner le propriétaire Luh PRO-PREE-Yĕ-TĕR

oysters les huîtres (f/pl) LA ZWEE-TRuh

P

package le paquet Luh Pah-Kĕ

paid payé PA-YA

pain la douleur Lah DOO-LouR

painting la peinture Lah PãÑ-TewR

pantyhose le collant Luh KO-LahÑ

paper le papier Luh Pah-PEE-A

park (to) stationner STah-SEE-O-NA

park le parc Luh PahRK

partner (business) associé ah-SO-SEE-A

party la soirée Lah SWah-RA

passenger le passager Luh Pah-Sah-ZHA

passport le passeport Luh PahS-POR

pasta les pâtes LA PahT

pastries les pâtisseries L@h P@h-T@-S@-B@

pen le stylo L@h ST@-L@

pencil le crayon L@h KB@-Y@ñ

pepper le poivre L@h PW@h-VB@h

perfume le parfum L@h P@B-F@ñ

person la personne L@h P@B-S@N

pharmacist le pharmacien

    L@h F@B-M@h-S@-@ñ

pharmacy la pharmacie L@h F@B-M@h-S@

phone book l'annuaire L@h-N@-@B

photo la photo L@ F@-T@

photographer le photographier

    L@h F@-T@-GB@h-F@-@

pie la tarte L@h T@hBT

pillow l'oreiller (m) L@-B@-Y@

pink rose B@Z

pizza la pizza L@h P@D-S@h

plastic le plastique L@h PL@hS-T@K

plate l'assiette (f) L@h-S@-@T

please s'il vous plaît S@L V@ PL@

pleasure le plaisir L🔤 PL🔤-Z🔤R

police la police L🔤 P🔤-L🔤S

police station la poste de police

L🔤 P🔤ST D🔤 P🔤-L🔤S

pork le porc L🔤 P🔤R

porter le porteur L🔤 P🔤R-T🔤R

post office la poste L🔤 P🔤ST

postcard la carte postale L🔤 K🔤RT P🔤S-T🔤L

potato la pomme de terre L🔤 P🔤M D🔤 T🔤R

pregnant enceinte 🔤ñ-S🔤ñT

prescription la prescription

L🔤 PR🔤-SKR🔤P-S🔤-🔤ñ

price le prix L🔤 PR🔤

problem le problème L🔤 PR🔤-BL🔤M

profession la profession L🔤 PR🔤-F🔤-S🔤-🔤N

public publique P🔤B-L🔤K

public telephone le téléphone publique

L🔤 T🔤-L🔤-F🔤N P🔤B-L🔤K

purified purifié P🔤R-🔤-F🔤-🔤

purple violet (m) V🔤-🔤-L🔤

violette (f) V🔤-🔤-L🔤T

purse le sac L🔤 S🔤K

Q

quality la qualité L@h K@h-L@-T@

question la question L@h K@S-T@-O@ñ

quickly rapidement B@h-P@D-M@hñ

quiet (be) taisez-vous T@-Z@ V@

quiet tranquille TB@hñ-K@L

R

radio la radio L@h B@hD-Y@

railroad le chemin de fer L@h SH@-M@ñ D@ F@B

rain la pluie L@h PL@-@

raincoat l'imperméable (m)

     L@ñ-P@B-M@-@B-L@

ramp la rampe L@h B@hMP

rare (cooked) saignant S@-NY@hñ

razor blades les lames de rasoir

     L@ L@hM D@ B@h-SW@hB

ready prêt PB@

receipt le reçu L@h B@h-S@

recommend (to) recommander

     B@h-K@-M@hñ-D@

red rouge B@ZH

repeat répéter B@-P@-T@

reservation la réservation

    Lah RA-ZÉR-Vah-SÉE-Oñ

restaurant le restaurant Luh RÉS-TO-Rahñ

return revenir Ruh-Vuh-NÉER

return (to give back) revenir Ruh-Vuh-NÉER

rice le riz Luh RÉE

rich riche RÉESH

right (correct) correct KO-RéKT

right (direction) à droite ah DRWahT

road le chemin Luh SHuh-Mäñ

room la chambre Lah SHahñ-BRuh

round trip l'aller et retour Lah-LA A Ruh-TooR

S

safe (hotel) le coffre-fort Luh KO-FRuh FOR

salad la salade Lah Sah-LahD

sale la vente Lah VahñT

salmon le saumon Luh Suh-MOñ

salt le sel Luh SéL

sandwich le sandwich Luh Sahñ-WÉECH

Saturday samedi Sah-Muh-DÉE

scissors les ciseaux (m) LA SÉE-ZO

sculpture la sculpture Lah SKewLP-TewR

seafood les fruits de mer (m)

LⒶ FRWⒺ DⓤⒽ MⒺR

season la saison LⒶⒽ SⒺ-ZⓄñ

seat la place LⒶⒽ PLⒶⒽS

secretary la secrétaire LⒶⒽ SⒺ-KRⒶ-TⒺR

section la section LⒶⒽ SⒺK-SⒺⒺ-ⓄⓄñ

September septembre SⒺP-TⒶⒽñ-BRⓤⒽ

service le service LⓤⒽ SⒺR-VⒺⒺS

several plusieurs PLⒺⓌ-ZYⓄⓌR

shampoo le shampooing LⓤⒽ SHⒶⒽñ-PⓄⓄ-ⒶN

sheets (bed) les draps LⒶ DRⒶⒽ

shirt la chemise LⒶⒽ SHⓤⒽ-MⒺⒺS

shoe la chaussure LⒶⒽ SHⓄ-SⒺⓌR

shoe store la boutique de chaussures

LⒶⒽ BⓄⓄ-TⒺⒺK DⓤⒽ SHⓄ-SⒺⓌR

shop la boutique LⒶⒽ BⓄⓄ-TⒺⒺK

shopping center le centre commercial

LⓤⒽ SⒶⒽñ-TRⓤⒽ KⓄ-MⒺR-SⒺ-ⒶⒽL

shower la douche LⒶⒽ DⓄⓄSH

shrimp les crevettes LⒶ KRⓤⒽ-VⒺT

sick malade MⒶⒽ-LⒶⒽD

sign (display) le signe LⓤⒽ SⒺⒺN-YⓤⒽ

signature la signature Lah SEEN-Yah-TewR

single seul Sou L

sir monsieur Muh-SYou

sister la soeur Lah SouR

size la taille Lah TA-You

skin la peau LA PO

skirt la jupe Lah ZHooP

sleeve la manche Lah MahñSH

slowly lentement Lahñ-Tuh-Mahñ

small petit (m) Puh-TEE

    petite (f) Puh-TEET

smile (to) sourire Soo-REER

smoke (to) fumer Few-MA

soap le savon Luh Sah-VOñ

socks les chaussettes LA SHO-SëT

some quelque KëL-Kuh

something quelque chose KëL-Kuh SHOZ

sometimes quelquefois KëL-Kuh-FWah

soon bientôt BEE-âñ-TO

sorry (I am) Je suis désolé

    ZHuh SWEE DA-SO-LA

soup la soupe Lah SooP

south   le sud   Lⓤⓗ   SⓔⓦD

souvenir   le souvenir   Lⓤⓗ   Sⓞⓞ-Vⓤⓗ-NⓔⓔR

speciality   la spécialité   Lⓐⓗ   SPⒶ-Sⓔⓔ-ⓐⓗ-Lⓔⓔ-TⒶ

spoon   la cuillère   Lⓐⓗ   KWⓔⓔ-ⓔR

spring (season)   le printemps   Lⓤⓗ   PRⓐñ-Tⓐⓗñ

stairs   les escaliers   LⒶ   Zⓔ-SKⓐⓗL-YⒶ

stamp   le timbre   Lⓤⓗ   Tⓐñ-BRⓤⓗ

station   la gare   Lⓐⓗ   GⓐⓗR

steak   le bifteck   Lⓤⓗ   BⓔⓔF-TⓔK

steamed   à l'etuvée   ⓐⓗ   LⒶ-Tⓔⓦ-VⒶ

stop   arrêtez   ⓐⓗ-Rⓔ-TⒶ

store   le magasin   Lⓤⓗ   Mⓐⓗ-Gⓐⓗ-Zⓐñ

straight ahead   tout droit   Tⓞⓞ   DRWⓐⓗ

strawberry   la fraise   Lⓐⓗ   FRⓔZ

street   la rue   Lⓐⓗ   Rⓔⓦ

string   la ficelle   Lⓐⓗ   Fⓔⓔ-SⓔL

subway   le métro   Lⓤⓗ   MⒶ-TRⓞ

sugar   le sucre   Lⓤⓗ   Sⓔⓦ-KRⓤⓗ

suit (clothes)   le complet   Lⓤⓗ   KⓄñ-PLⓔ

suitcase   la valise   Lⓐⓗ   Vⓐⓗ-LⓔⓔS

summer   l'été   LⒶ-TⒶ

sun le soleil Lⓤⓗ Sⓞ-LⒶ

Sunday dimanche DⒺⒺ-MⓐⓗñSH

sunglasses les lunettes de soleil (f/pl)

　　LⒶ Lⓔⓦ-Nⓔ̂T Dⓤⓗ Sⓞ-LⒶ

suntan lotion la lotion à bronzer

　　Lⓐⓗ Lⓞ-SⒺⒺ-Oñ ⓐⓗ BBⓞñ-ZⒶ

supermarket le supermarché

　　Lⓤⓗ Sⓔⓦ-Pⓔ̂R-MⓐⓗR-SHⒶ

surprise la surprise Lⓐⓗ SⓔⓦR-PRⒺⒺZ

sweet doux Dⓞⓞ

swim (to) nager Nⓐⓗ-ZHⒶ

swimming pool la piscine Lⓐⓗ PⒺⒺ-SⒺⒺN

synagogue la synagogue Lⓐⓗ SⒺⒺ-Nⓐⓗ-GⓞG

T

table la table Lⓐⓗ Tⓐⓗ-BLⓤⓗ

tampons les tampons LⒶ Tⓐⓗñ-POñ

tape (sticky) le ruban Lⓤⓗ Rⓔⓦ-Bⓐⓗñ

tape recorder le magnétophone

　　Lⓤⓗ Mⓐⓗ-NⒶ-Tⓞ-Fⓞ N

tax la taxe Lⓐⓗ TⓐⓗKS

taxi le taxi L(uh) T(a)K-S(ee)

tea le thé L(uh) T(a)

telegram le télégramme L(uh) T(a)-L(a)-GR(ah)M

telephone le téléphone L(uh) T(a)-L(a)-F(o)N

television la télévision L(ah) T(a)-L(a)-V(ee)-S(ee)-O(ñ)

temperature la température

    L(ah) T(ah)ñ-P(e)-R(ah)-T(ew)R

temple le temple L(uh) T(ah)ñ-PL(uh)

tennis la tennis L(ah) T(e)-N(ee)S

tennis court le terrain de tennis

    L(uh) T(e)-R(a)ñ D(uh) T(e)-N(ee)S

thank you merci M(e)R-S(ee)

that cela S(uh)-L(ah)

the le (m) L(uh)

    la (f) L(ah)

theater le théâtre L(uh) T(a)-(ah)-TR(uh)

there là L(ah)

they ils (ee)L

this ce / cet / cette S(uh) / S(e)T / S(e)T

thread le fil L(uh) F(ee)L

throat la gorge L(ah) G(o)RZH

Thursday jeudi ZH(ou)-D(ee)

ticket le billet Luh BEE-YA

tie la cravate Lah KRah-Vah-T

time l'heure LooR

tip (gratuity) le pourboire Luh PooR-BWahR

tire (car) le pneu Luh Puh-Nou

tired fatigué Fah-TEE-GA

toast pain grillé Pahñ GREE-YA

tobacco le tabac Luh Tah-Bah

today aujourd'hui O-ZHooR-DWEE

toe l'orteil LOR-TA

together ensemble ahñ-Sahñ-BLuh

toilet la toilette Lah TWah-LeT

toilet paper le papier hygiénique

   Luh Pah-PEE-A EE-ZHEE-A-NEEK

tomato la tomate Lah TO-MahT

tomorrow demain Duh-Mahñ

toothache le mal aux dents Luh MahL O Dahñ

toothbrush la brosse à dents

   Lah BROS ah Dahñ

toothpaste le dentifrice Luh Dahñ-TEE-FREES

toothpick le cure-dents Luh KewR Dahñ

tour la visite Lah VEE-ZEET

tourist le touriste L⒰ T⍟-Ⓡ⒠ST

tourist office le bureau de tourisme

L⒰ B⒠w-Ⓡ⍟ D⒰ T⍟-Ⓡ⒠S-M⒰

towel la serviette L⒜ S⒠R-V⒠-⒠T

train le train L⒰ TⒷ⒜ñ

travel agency l'agence de voyage

L⒜-ZH⒜ñS D⒰ VW⒜-Y⒜ZH

traveler's check le chèque de voyage

L⒰ SHⒺK D⒰ VW⒜-Y⒜ZH

trip le voyage L⒰ VW⒜-Y⒜ZH

trousers le pantalon L⒰ P⒜ñ-T⒜-L⍟ñ

trout la truite L⒜ TⒷW⒠w-⒠⒠T

truth la vérité L⒜ V⒜-Ⓡ⒠-T⒜

Tuesday mardi M⒜R-D⒠⒠

turkey la dinde L⒜ D⒜ñND

U

umbrella la parapluie L⒜ P⒜-Ⓡ⒜-PL⒠w-⒠⒠

understand (to) comprendre K⍟N-PⓇ⒜ñ-DⒷ⒰

underwear les sous-vêtements

L⒜ S⍟⍟ VⒺT-M⒜ñ

United Kingdom Royaume-Uni

Ⓡ⍟y-⍟⍟M ⍟⍟-N⒠⒠

United States les Etats-Unis

LⒶ ZⒶ-Tⓐⓗ-Zⓔⓦ-NⒺ

university l'université (f) Lⓔⓦ-NⒺ-VⓔⓇ-SⒺ-TⒶ

up haut Ⓞ

urgent urgent ⓔⓦR-ZHⓐⓗñ

V

vacancies (accommodation) chambres libres (f/pl)

SHⓐⓗñ-BRⓤⓗ LⒺ-BRⓤⓗ

vacation les vacances LⒶ Vⓐⓗ-KⓐⓗñS

valuable précieux (m) PRⒶ-SYⓞⓤ

précieuse (f) PRⒶ-SYⓞⓤS

value le valeur Lⓤⓗ Vⓐⓗ-LⓞⓤR

vanilla la vanille Lⓐⓗ Vⓐⓗ-NⒺ

veal le veau Lⓤⓗ VⓄ

vegetables les légumes (m) LⒶ LⒶ-GⓔⓦM

view la vue Lⓐⓗ Vⓔⓦ

vinegar le vinaigre Lⓤⓗ VⒺ-NⒶ-GRⓤⓗ

voyage le voyage Lⓤⓗ VWⓐⓗ-YⓐⓗZH

W

wait attendez ⓐⓗ-Tⓐⓗñ-DⒶ

waiter le garçon Lⓤⓗ GⓐⓗR-SOñ

waitress la serveuse Lⓐⓗ SⓔⓇ-VⓞⓤS

want (I) Je voudrais ZHⓤ V◎-DⓇⒶ

wash (to) laver Lⓐ-VⒶ

watch (time piece) la montre Lⓐ M◎ñ-TⓇⓤ

watch out! attention ⓐ-Tⓐñ-SⒺ-Oñ

water l'eau L◎

we nous N◎◎

weather le temps Lⓤ Tⓐñ

Wednesday mercredi MⒺⓇ-KⓇⓤ-DⒺ

week la semaine Lⓐ Sⓤ-MⒺN

weekend le week-end Lⓤ WⒺK-ⒺND

welcome bienvenu BⒺ-ⓐñ-VⒺ-Nⓔ

well done (cooked) bien cuit BⒺ-ⓐñ KWⒺ

west l'ouest L◎-ⒺST

what? que? / quoi? Kⓤ / KWⓐ

wheelchair le fauteuil roulant

    Lⓤ F◎-T◎-Y◎ Ⓡ◎-Lⓐñ

when? quand? Kⓐñ

where? où? ◎

which? quel? / quelle KⒺL

white blanc (m) BLⓐñ / blanche (f) BLⓐñSH

who? qui? KⒺ

why? pourquoi? POOR-KWah

wife la femme Lah FAM

wind le vent Luh Vahñ

window la fenêtre Lah Fuh-NÊ-TRuh

wine le vin Luh Vañ

wine list la carte de vins Lah KahRT Duh Vañ

winter l'hiver LEE-VêR

with avec ah-VêK

woman la femme Lah FahM

wonderful merveilleux MêR-VA-You

world le monde Luh MOñD

wrong avoir tort uh-VWahR TOR

XYZ

year l'année Lah-NA

yellow jaune ZHON

yes oui WEE

yesterday hier YêR

you tu / vous Tew / Voo

zipper la fermeture Lah FêR-Muh-TewR

zoo le zoo Luh ZO

EASILY PRONOUNCED
LANGUAGE SYSTEMS

Author Clyde Peters graduated from Radford High School and the University of Hawaii and has traveled the world as a travel writer. His innovative Say It Right phrase books have revolutionized the way languages are taught and learned. Mr. Peters invented the Vowel Symbol System for easy and correct pronunciation of virtually any language. He currently continues traveling the world working on new languages and divides his spare time between Las Vegas, Nevada, and Hawaii.

Betty Chapman is a successful business woman who along with Mr. Peters founded Easily Pronounced Language Systems to promote education, travel, and custom tailored language solutions. "Moving beyond expectation to acquisition and accomplishment is possible with EPLS."

Priscilla Leal Bailey is the senior series editor for all Say It Right products and has proved indispensable in editing and implementing the EPLS Vowel Symbol System. We are forever grateful for her belief and support.

SAY IT RIGHT SERIES
Infinite Destinations
One Pronunciation System!

Audio Editions

Say It Right App on iTunes

THANKS!

The nicest thing you can say to anyone in any language is "Thank you." Try some of these languages using the incredible EPLS Vowel Symbol System.

Arabic
SH⊚-KR@N

Chinese
SH℮℮́ SH℮℮̃

French
M℮R-S℮℮

German
D@N-Kⓤ

Hawaiian
M@-H@́-L◎

Italian
GR@T-S℮℮-℮̃

Japanese
D◎-M◎

Portuguese
◎-BR℮℮-G@́-D◎

Russian
SP@-S℮℮-B@

Spanish
GR@́-S℮℮-@S

Swahili
@-S@́N-T④

Tagalog
S@-L@́-M@T

INDEX

QUICK REFERENCE PAGE

Hello
Bonjour
BOñ ZHOOB

Good-bye
Au revoir
O Buh-VWahB

How are you?
Comment allez-vous?
KO-MOñ Tah-LA-Voo

Fine / Very well
Très bien
TBA BEE-āN

Yes
Oui
WEE

No
Non
NOñ

Please
S'il vous plaît
SEEL Voo PLē

Thank you
Merci
MĒB-SEE

I would like...
Je voudrais...
ZHuh Voo-DBA...

Where is...
Où est...
oo A...

I don't understand!
Je ne comprends pas!
ZHuhN-uh KOñ-PBahñ Pah

Help!
Au secours!
O Suh-KooB